A Curriculum of Imagination in an Era of Standardization

*An Imaginative Dialogue
with Maxine Greene and Paulo Freire*

A volume in
Landscapes of Education
William H. Schubert and Ming Fang He, *Series Editors*

A Curriculum of Imagination in an Era of Standardization

*An Imaginative Dialogue
with Maxine Greene and Paulo Freire*

Robert Lake

Georgia Southern University

INFORMATION AGE PUBLISHING, INC.
Charlotte, NC • www.infoagepub.com

Library of Congress Cataloging-in-Publication Data

Lake, Robert (Robert Lewis), 1951-
  A curriculum of imagination in an era of standardization : an imaginative
dialogue / with Maxine Greene and Paulo Freire.
      pages cm – (Landscapes of Education.)
  Includes bibliographical references.
  ISBN 978-1-62396-265-4 (pbk.) – ISBN 978-1-62396-266-1 (hardcover) –
ISBN 978-1-62396-267-8 (ebook) 1. Creative thinking. 2. Greene, Maxine.
3. Freire, Paulo, 1921-1997. I. Title.
  LB1062.L34 2013
  370.15'7–dc23

                                                        2013006340

Dedication

This book is dedicated first and foremost to my wife Elizabeth. You are a walking embodiment of a curriculum of imagination, who has awakened me to find beauty in so much of what continually surrounds us. Secondly, I dedicate this work to my six children, Rachel, John, Thomas, David, Mary Elizabeth, and William. You each have your own distinct perspective, interests, and expression. Through you I have learned to treasure the uniqueness of the entire human family. This work is also dedicated to my grandchildren, Lily Rose, Liam, Juniper, Carson, and those yet to come. May imagination enable you to always live above walls.

Contents

Series Foreword

Landscapes of Education

In this book series, we explore panoramic landscapes of education. We invite a wide array of authors from diverse theoretical traditions and geographical locations around the world to ponder deeply and critically undulating and evolving contours of educational experience. We perceive contours of educational experience as landscapes that cultivate and are cultivated by who we were and how we become who we are as individuals and as humanity (Nussbaum, 1997). We engage with complex hills and rift valleys, rocky roads and serene pathways, war torn terrains and flowering gardens, towering trees and wuthering grasses, jagged cliffs and unyielding rocks, flowing rivers and uneven oceans evolving with flows of life that shape our perspectives, modify our ideas, and forge our actions. Building upon John Dewey's (1916) democratic conception of education and William Schubert's (2009) ideals of love, justice, and education, we perceive landscapes of education not only as schools but also as gathering places (Dewey, 1933) for humans to pursue worthwhile living. We honor the poetics of landscapes of education flourishing with divergence, convergence, diversity, and complexity of experience.

We look for authors who can move in new directions. We open dialogue on educational issues and situations of shared concerns. We create a space for educational workers such as public intellectuals, scholars, artists, and practitioners to engage in inquiries into education drawn from multiple perspectives such as art, music, language, literature, philosophy, history, so-

A Curriculum of Imagination in an Era of Standardization, pages xi–xvi
Copyright © 2013 by Information Age Publishing

cial sciences, and professional studies. We welcome cross-disciplinary, inter-disciplinary, trans-disciplinary, and counter-disciplinary work. We look for possibilities that are fresh and poetic, nuanced and novelistic, theoretical and practical, personal and political, imaginative and improvisational.

We expand parameters of educational inquiry substantively and methodologically. Substantively, books in this series explore multifarious landscapes wherever education occurs. Such explorations provocatively portray education in schools, workplaces, nonschool settings, and relationships. Methodologically, we encourage diverse forms of inquiry drawing on a wide array of research traditions, approaches, methods, and techniques such as ethnomethodology, phenomenology, hermeneutics, feminism, rhizomatics, deconstructionism, grounded theory, case studies, survey studies, interviews, participant observation, action research, teacher research, activist feminist inquiry, self study, life history, teacher lore, autobiography, biography, memoir, documentary studies, art-based inquiry, ethnography/critical ethnography, autoethnography, participatory inquiry, narrative inquiry, fiction, cross-cultural and multicultural narrative inquiry, psychoanalysis, queer inquiry, and personal~passionate~participatory inquiry.

We also feature works that amplify the educational value of mass media such as movies, DVDs, television, the Internet, comics, news comedy, cell phones, My Space and Face Book, videos, videogames, computers, and the World Wide Web. We hope to explore how we learn through such electronic frontiers in vastly new ways with little tutelage. We hope to encourage creative improvising, problem posing, critical inquiring, and joyful learning illuminated in these new ways of learning though electronic frontiers which are often suppressed and repressed in schooling. We hope to acknowledge the power of human beings to learn without lesson plans, manuals, worksheets, standardized tests, acquisitive rewards, or external standards.

We encourage expansions that move beyond Western orthodoxies to embrace landscapes from the Eastern (Asian), Southern (African and Latin American), and Oceanic (islandic) worlds. We especially want to see renditions move into third spaces (Gutiérrez, Rymes, & Larson, 1995) and in-between (He, 2003, 2010) that push boundaries, shift borders, dissolve barriers, and thrive upon contradictions of life. It is our intention that the works featured in this series reveal more of the world-wide landscapes of cultures, ideas, and practices that transgress dominant Western ideologies and their corporate and colonizing legacies. These works have potential in developing transcendent theories of decolonization (e.g., Tuhiwai Smith, 2001), advocating the liberty of indigenous language, cultural rights, and intellectualism (e.g., Grande, 2004), shattering monocultures of the mind

(Shiva, 1993), overcoming perils of globalization, and inventing a better human condition for all.

We also highlight activist and social justice oriented research (e.g., Ayers, Quinn, & Stovall, 2009) and personal~passionate~participatory inquiry (e.g., He & Phillion, 2008) that engage participation of all citizens, encourage respect, innovation, interaction, cohesion, justice, and peace, and promote cultural, linguistic, intellectual, and ecological diversity and complexity. We celebrate postcolonial feminist work (e.g., Minh-ha, 1989; Mohanty, 2003/2005; Narayan, 1997) that explores migration, slavery, suppression, resistance, representation, difference, race, gender, place and responses to influential discourses of racism, sexism, classism, and colonialism. We also feature ecofeminist inquiry that explores the intersectionality of repatri-archal historical analysis, spirituality, racism, classism, imperialism, heterosexism, ageism, ableism, anthropocentrism, speciesism, and other forms of oppression (Mies & Shiva, 1993).

Books in this series focus on the what, why, how, when, where, and for whom of relationships, interactions, and transactions that transform human beings to different levels of awareness to build communities and public spaces with shared interests and common goals to strive for equitable, just, and invigorating human conditions. We seek explorations of the educational aspects of relationships (e.g., family, friendship), international, transnational, or intercultural understanding (e.g., exile, diaspora, displacement, indigenous knowledge), and circumstances of living (e.g., poverty, racism, alienation, war, colonization, oppression, and globalization). We want to see how languages, literacies, communities, homes, and families shape images of life's mysteries and events (Ulich, 1955), such as love, tradition, birth, death, success or failure, hopes of salvation, or immortality. These educational dimensions of life dynamically influence and are influenced by life in and out of schools (Schubert, 2010) and in-between (He, 2003, 2010). Through engaging such pursuits, this book series illuminates how human beings improvise lives (Bateson, 1989) and commitments in diverse, complicated, and often contested landscapes of education.

Unlike more definitively crafted book series that explicate inclusions and exclusions with ease and precision, our invitations continuously expand. The depths and breadths of landscapes where we live surpass everyday gaze and complicate static analysis. We showcase books that bring a sense of wonder and surprise, make the strange familiar and the familiar strange, and evoke what we do not expect. We do not narrow or define the topics of this series. Rather, we open doors to new perspectives, diverse paradigms, and creative possibilities. We invite authors to surprise us with their insightful ideas of what has been, what is, and what might be. For this volume, Robert Lake has surprised us with an inspiring compilation of explorations on what a curriculum of imagination can teach us about education, inquiry, and life.

The landscape of education continues to be under siege outside-in and inside-out: "turning over public assets and spaces to private management; dismantling and opposing independent and collective voice of teachers; reducing education to a single narrow metric" (Ayers, 2012); schooling to follow order and for profit through throat cutting competitions, acquisitive test scores, and commodified standards (Schubert, 2009). We face a moment in life that demands educational workers with epistemological, institutional, geographical, experiential, and methodological diversity to exile voluntarily (He, 2010) from commodified (Illich, 1970; Reynolds & Webber, 2009), acquisitive (Schubert, 2009), and deskilling (Apple, 1986) policy and practice; to cultivate radical imagination (e.g., Anyon, 2005; Freire, 2007; Giroux, 2007; Greene, 1995) and educated hope (Giroux, 2007; Harvey, 2000,) and to politicize possibilities (Olson & Worsham, 2007) to thrive with unsettling and troubling aspects of lives (Saïd, 1994, 2003) without romanticizing or cynicizing the world where we live; to raise challenging questions, transcend inquiry boundaries, transgress orthodoxy and dogma, research silenced narratives of underrepresented or disenfranchised individuals and groups with hearts and minds; to fight back all forms of suppression, repression, and oppression; and to promote a more balanced and equitable human condition that embodies cultural, linguistic, and ecological diversity and plurality of individuals, groups, tribes, and societies that is conducive to the flourishing of creative capacities that invigorate intellectual, emotional, moral, and spiritual existence for all.

— **William H. Schubert**
Ming Fang He

References

Anyon, J. (2005). *Radical possibilities: Public policy, urban education, and a new social movement.* New York, NY: Routledge.

Apple, M. (1986). *Teachers and texts: A political economy of class and gender relations in education.* New York, NY: Routledge & Kegan Paul.

Ayers, W. (2012). *An open letter to President Obama.* Retrieved on November 17, 2012 at http://www.good.is/posts/an-open-letter-to-president-obama-from-bill-ayers.

Ayers, W., Quinn, T., & Stovall, D. (Eds.) (2009). *Handbook of social justice in education.* New York, NY: Routledge.

Bateson, M. C. (1989). *Composing a life.* New York, NY: The Atlantic Monthly Press.

Dewey, J. (1916). *Democracy and education.* New York, NY: Macmillan.

Dewey, J. (1933). Dewey outlines utopian schools. *New York Times*, April 23, p. 7. Also in Boydston, J. A. (Ed.), *The later works (1925–1953) of John Dewey*, Volume 9, (pp. 136–140) Carbondale, IL: Southern Illinois University Press, 1989.

Freire, P. (2007). *Daring to dream: Toward a pedagogy of the unfinished.* Organized and presented by Ana Maria Araújo Freire. Forewords by Peter Park and Ana Lúcia Souza De Freitas. Boulder, CO: Paradigm.

Giroux, H. (2007). When the darkness comes and hope is subversive (Foreword). In G. A. Olson & L. Worsham (Eds.), *The politics of possibility: Encountering the radical imagination* (pp. vii–xviii). Boulder, CO: Paradigm.

Grande, S. (2004). *Red pedagogy: Native American social and political thought.* New York, NY: Rowman & Littlefield.

Greene, M. (1995). *Releasing the imagination: Essays on education, the arts, and social change.* San Francisco: Jossey-Bass.

Gutiérrez, K. D., Rymes, B., & Larson, J. (1995). Script, counterscript, and underlife in the classroom: James Brown versus Brown v. Board of Education. *Harvard Educational Review, 65*(3), 445–471.

Harvey, D. (2000). *Spaces of hope.* Berkeley, CA: University of California Press.

He, M. F. (2003). *A river forever flowing: Cross-cultural lives and identities in the multicultural landscape.* Greenwich, CT: Information Age Publishers.

He, M. F. (2010). Exile pedagogy: Teaching in-between. In J. A. Sandlin, B. D. Schultz, & J. Burdick (Eds.), *Handbook of public pedagogy* (pp. 469–482). New York, NY: Routledge.

He, M. F., & Phillion, J. (2008). *Personal~passionate~participatory inquiry into social justice in education.* Charlotte, NC: Information Age Publishing.

Illich, I. (1970). *De-schooling society.* New York, NY: Harper and Row.

Mies, M., & Shiva, S. (1993). *Ecofeminism.* Halifax, Nova Scotia, Canada: Fernwood.

Minh-Ha, T. T. (1989). *Woman, native, other: Writing postcoloniality and feminism* (Midland Books). Bloomington, IN: Indiana University Press.

Mohanty, C. T. (2003/2005). *Feminism without borders: Decolonizing theory, practicing solidarity.* Durham, NC: Duke University Press.

Narayan, U. (1997). *Dislocating cultures: Identities, traditions, and third world feminism.* New York, NY: Routledge.

Nussbaum, M. (1997). *Cultivating humanity: A classical defense of reform in liberal education.* Cambridge, MA: Harvard University Press.

Olson, G. A., & Worsham, L. (Eds.). (2007). *The poslitics of possibility: Encountering the radical imagination.* Boulder, CO: Paradigm.

Reynolds, W., & Webber, Julie A. (2009). *The civic Gospel: A political cartography of Christianity.* Rotterdam/Boston/Taipei: Sense.

Saïd, E. W. (1994). *Representations of the intellectual.* New York, NY: Vintage Books.

Saïd, E. W. (2003). *Reflections on exile and other essays (Convergences: Inventories of the Present).* Cambridge, MA: Harvard University Press.

Schubert, W. H. (2009). *Love, justice, and education: John Dewey and the Utopians.* Charlotte, NC: Information Age Publishing.

Schubert, W. H. (2010). Outside curriculum. In C. Kridel (Ed.), *Encyclopedia of curriculum studies* (pp. 624–628). Thousand Oaks, CA: Sage.

Shiva, V. (1993). *Monocultures of the mind: Perspectives on biodiversity and biotechnology.* Atlantic Highlands, NJ: Zed Books.

Tuhiwai Smith, L. (2001). *Decolonizing methodologies: Research and indigenous peoples.* London: Zed Books.

Ulich, R. (1955). Response to Ralph Harper's essay. In N. B. Henry. (Ed.), *Modern philosophies of education, Fifty-fourth Yearbook (Part I) of the National Society for the Study of Education* (pp. 254–257). Chicago: University of Chicago Press.

Acknowledgements

I want to express my deep gratitude to Dr. Ming Fang He for giving me the idea of rendering "an intellectual conversation between Maxine Greene and Paulo Freire." Dr. He, you have been a source of continual inspiration to me as a caring mentor and an outstanding and tireless scholar who is never static in her pursuit of understanding. I have learned much about metaphor in personal narrative from you! Thank you for all of your help!

Thank you, William Reynolds, for introducing me to the work of Paulo Freire and for demonstrating his approach to teaching without reducing it to a method; I also acknowledge your vast contribution to my understanding of curriculum as "being." I also want to thank Clyde Coreil for always being a "muse of fire" concerning imagination through our many telephone conversations. Your passion and breadth of understanding of this topic convinced me that I needed to carry on your legacy. Thank you, William Schubert, for your wonderful advice, critique, collegiality, inspiration and logistical support in getting this book published. I am very grateful to our graduate assistants Amber Bryan and Quinnell Lea Chay Vasser for their superb help in copy editing. Last but not least I want to acknowledge the life and work of Maxine Greene. Her writing has become a voice in my head, "lighting the slow fuse of the possible!"

Prologue

Imagination lies at a kind of crux where perception, memory,
idea generation, emotion, metaphor, and no doubt other labeled features
of our lives, intersect and interact
—Egan, 1992, p. 3

This book explores ways of seeing, knowing, and learning that are frequently excluded in this present climate of standardized practices in the field of education. In particular, I explore how imagination permeates every aspect of life experience and helps develop personal and political awareness in students to look beyond what they take for granted, to question the normal, and to develop various ways of knowing, seeing, feeling, and creating positive social and educational change in this time of increasing standardization in the entire global culture. By drawing upon the historical and contemporary evolution of the concepts of imagination and metaphor, I explore how they make possible the creation of personal meaning and agency.

Another distinguishing feature of this work is that it is framed upon an "imaginary" dialogue that uses actual quotations from Maxine Greene and Paulo Freire, with personal commentary and citations from others interspersed at various points in the conversation. The study also explores the connection between eugenics and the origin of standardized testing and the practice of tracking in the United States during the 20th century. By reflecting on my own experience as a student, teacher, and researcher, I look for ways to describe the roles of imagination in naming, being, and transforming private and public worlds. I also focus on the significance of sensing gaps and perceiving the unanswered, the unfinished, and the un-

---

A Curriculum of Imagination in an Era of Standardization, pages xix–xxxv
Copyright © 2013 by Information Age Publishing
xix

just in ways that passionately move us beyond the taken-for-granted and the status quo in the present system of "official knowledge" and contrived practices of classroom accountability.

The doorway to the personal construction of meaning lies in imagination, for it is out of this uniquely human endowment that connections are made between experience and the creation of new ideas. One of the greatest functions of imagination is that it "brings severed parts together" (Greene, 1995, p. 99). The marvel of this is that the joined parts may look to others to be completely unrelated, and yet to the imaginer, they are one. For example, what is the connection between algae and fuel for the internal combustion engine or between a guitar solo and a percentage problem in math? The answer to both these questions has the potential to remove the kind of fragmented knowledge and the formidable "walls" between content area subjects that comprised the curriculum of the aristocracy of Europe over 200 years ago at the height of the age of Colonialism. In the domain of education, the legacy of that period is still very much alive. Although imagination operates in the innermost areas of learning, it is often treated as fanciful, "off the deep end," or not "relevant" in the present climate of highly scripted classroom procedures and practices.

This inquiry traces the evolution of the concept of imagination and seeks connections to contemporary curriculum theory through both creative and critical applications. In particular, I reflect on historical and contemporary definitions of imagination and metaphor and how they enable the creation of personal meaning and agency. Metaphoric relationships are explored in greater depth by considering their role in "sensing gaps" and problem finding in creative and critical thinking. I also provide a wide range of applications and connections to practice from a variety of settings.

The Era of Standardization

The time that we now live in is one that welcomes known quantity and homogeneity of both production and end product. Quantifiable uniformity is embraced, and divergent thinking is portrayed as weakness. The operative words under these prevailing conditions are "accountability," "benchmarks," and "performance standards." These buzzwords have entered the field of education through the world of business, technology, and industry and, for the most part, have driven the configuration of schooling at every level since the age of mass production began in the early 20th century.

In a time when changes in technology occur at an alarming pace and there is a demand for deep and specialized understanding and experience in so many fields of inquiry, educational practices are increasingly dominated by the industrial model of measurable "efficiency" through officially prescribed modes of adherence to highly scripted curricular practices, "norms," and other "performance-based" indicators. These conditions have left little room for the kind of creative and critical thinking that embraces personal meaning or that welcomes the kind of thickly described multiplicity of perspectives that are essential to release minds from the status quo in every domain, including science, math, and literacy, as well as the sociopolitical and the philosophical fields of inquiry. It is in this context that I seek to discover ways that imagination can take us beyond these prevailing standardized practices.

In 2010, trends toward standardized outcomes in education are at an all-time high. The recent expansion of the No Child Left Behind (U.S. Department of Education, 2005) policy to the present iteration of *Race to the Top* (U.S. Department of Education, 2009) has opened the door to a nationally standardized curriculum. The accompanying legislation to both these educational policies marks the first time in our history that the receipt of federal funds for education is based on performance measures on standardized tests.

One of the most profound injustices to this is that students must align to the same benchmarks in spite of their vast differences in socio-economic status, physical ability or limited English proficiency. According to the official website of the United States Department of Education (2005), "A critical change in measuring performance under No Child Left Behind is that schools must disaggregate the data so that all student groups—including poor and minority students, students with limited English proficiency, and students with disabilities are measured" (p. 2).

This change will, more than likely, widen the gap between students who are naturally suited to taking tests and those whose abilities might be discovered by other means. The reduction of knowledge to the retrieval of facts on multiple choice tests often keeps the student from making the vital to distinguishing "construction of meaning from the processing of information" (Modell, 2003, p. 9). This distinction is vital to the future of a culture that is in the throes of the information age.

To illustrate the ineffectiveness of the effects of standardized schooling, I draw the results of a recent report from the NEAP 2010: The data show a flat line in terms of any improvement in reading scores for 8th graders from 1992–2009. The sweeping changes in 2002 netted no significant improvement in test scores for this period. Tragically, this age group is not a priority for the educational policymakers who comprise the National Reading

Panel. This group plays a major role in shaping the literacy components of the No Child Left Behind Act of 2003.

The largest share of funding is going to the Reading First initiative, which "builds upon [the National Reading Panel's] findings by investing in scientifically-based reading instruction programs in the early grades" (U.S. Department of Education, 2001, p. 10). Middle-school-aged children need help beyond fluency instruction. It is the early teen years that students need the kind of teaching that fosters reading for higher order thinking and critical literacy. This is the domain of the imagination. The following statistics from a 35-year-long nationwide study reflect this need:

> The performance of 17-year-olds on the 2008 reading and mathematics assessments was not measurably different from their performance in the early 1970s. The average reading score for 17-year-olds was higher in 2008 than in 2004 but was not significantly different from the score in 1971. In mathematics, the average score for 17-year-olds in 2008 was not significantly different from the scores in either 2004 or 1973. (Rampey, Dion, & Donahue, 2009, p. 479)

In spite of claims of inclusion and "progress" for all, these statistics are being used to justify cultural irresponsibility. Tracking has always been based on statistical outcomes, and though the labels for it are changed every few years, standardized tests are used as a means of reinforcing the stratification of our culture. As Sacks (1999) suggests in his book *Standardized Minds,* this hegemonic control is maintained by the use of the weasel word "merit":

> Most people would agree that, in a democracy, merit is a good basis for deciding who gets ahead. The rub is how you define merit. We have settled on a system that defines merit in large part as the "potential" to achieve according to test results. It turns out that the lion's share of the potential in our society goes to those with well-to-do, highly educated parents. The aristocracy also used to perpetuate itself on the basis of birth and parentage. But the nation's elites now perpetuate their class privilege with rules of their own making that have persisted for several decades, rules legitimated and protected by a pseudoscientific objectivity. (p. 15)

One way that the concept of meritocracy plays out is in the area of middle school math education. In the eighth grade especially, algebraic concepts are introduced that have proven to be the great divide between the college track in high school and technical education. This is often because unqualified teachers are hired by schools in poorer districts and, of course, there is a direct correlation between math success and teacher qualification (Parmalee, Coble, & Swanson, 1985, pp. 13-15). In spite of these deplorable conditions, some children are able to find their own way out, mostly by what they learn outside the classroom. I am one such example.

Singing Over Walls: My Autobiographical Roots

My quest to understand a curriculum of imagination springs out of the experiences I had in my childhood. As I look back on my earliest years and up to this present moment, it is now crystal clear to me that many of the richest and most educative experiences took place outside of the formal classroom environment in ways that I can now recognize as a personally constructed curriculum of imagination. I will begin my story with the day that my father went to my meet my mother's family.

"Now Charley, you can put that ax down! I love your daughter and will take good care of her," my father said. "I won't let you take away my best worker," was my grandfather's reply. Eventually my dad talked Charley Gainey into putting down the ax, and he took my mother away from a North Carolina sharecropper's home to live in Tecumseh, Michigan. My mother came from a family of eleven brothers and sisters and started working in the cotton fields with all of them when she was five years old. My father had been stationed nearby at Fort Bragg, North Carolina during the Second World War. My mother finished the seventh grade and my father finished the eighth grade. My paternal grandfather served as a migrant laborer in logging camps that stretched from Northern Michigan to Saskatchewan, Canada, and he would leave home for months at a time. After World War II, my father found work in a refrigeration compressor factory, where he worked for thirty years, and another part time job in a wooden pallet factory. While I was growing up, my mother was a waitress in small restaurants, serving locals and truckers. We were considered "the working poor." Now, as I consider my family background and school experiences, I can clearly see them as the source of my passion for responsive and imaginative teaching for social justice.

I still remember the wooden outhouse that that all our family used for part of my earliest years. At least we had running cold water in the house, so water for baths had to be heated on the stove. My sisters took the first baths, and I got their leftover bath water because I played outside as much as possible and got the dirtiest.

I received three D's in kindergarten and was placed in "group two" in first-grade reading. I was a "hyperactive" child who had a very hard time sitting still for too long. I found school to be mostly quite boring with few exceptions. I really did enjoy "story time," personal narrative in history, and most of the non-grammar aspects of English and music, although you would not be able to get a clear assessment of that from my grade transcripts. I learned many things on my own through creative playing and exploration. I remember when I was around nine years old that I brought two spoons to a room in our basement where all of canned food was kept. I would tap each jar with a spoon to hear the tone each one created and add or remove water to tune each one and then line them up to play simple songs. As I look back, this kind of play was fundamental to finding my own voice and personal agency later on in life.

At one point in high school, I remember being placed in social studies for "slow" readers, general math, and industrial arts because of standardized tests results. I simply did not test well, especially after my parents' divorce. That point in my life left me feeling like my whole world was ripped apart. This situation is so common today, yet for millions of people, the effects on their lives are similar if not much worse.

One day a caring teacher came as a substitute to "slow readers" social studies. He told me that I did not belong there and placed me in his World History class. I still continued to do poorly in school, but I will never forget that teacher. I have sought to model his example in looking past the numbers with my own students.

My passion for cultivating multiple literacies came out of my own experiences with music. At the same time that I was having such a struggle as a high school student, outside of school, I began to flourish as a musician. One strongly defining moment took place in my second year of high school. I remember hearing a song by the Lovin' Spoonful (1965) featuring a harmonica solo by John Sebastian called *Night Owl Blues*. I was so drawn in by the emotional tone and skill expressed in that song that I said to myself, "I will learn to play just like that!" A few months later, I could play most of it! Not long after that, I was asked to play in a band. My level of self-confidence was altered considerably.

Fast forward through several garage bands and later accompanying myself on the guitar, to the time I met my wife Elizabeth. She once confessed that she married me "because I was nice and played the guitar." On several occasions we lived with her parents. Her father was a lawyer and her mother was an art teacher, and their home was rich with academic language and books. By daily interaction in that environment and with my auditory style of learning, I found myself thinking, speaking, reading, and writing much more expansively in ways that brought positive changes in my view of myself as a person and life partner, as well as a father and teacher.

It fact it was through music that I began my teaching career, by teaching English through songs to ESL students. For more than twelve years, I worked as a teacher of English for immigrant children and adults, high school dropouts preparing for the GED, and developmental reading students at a technical college. With all these students, I have witnessed the effects of cultural, social, and academic marginalization and exclusion. My work with these groups drove my passion for relevant teaching even further as I looked for ways to help them move beyond both academic and social obstacles and into personal agency. The aspect of teaching that has worked the best with all these students can be described as culturally sensitive participation that seeks to nurture each student's personal voice by helping them connect to the abilities and understanding that they already possess and inspiring in them a spirit of exploration.

Why I Chose to Write About Imagination

My passion to understand what is meant by imagination has increased throughout my life as both a student and a teacher for many reasons. One is because I see the tragic effects of unimaginative schooling on our culture as a result of the increasingly standardized and highly scripted practices in the field of education. Another reason is that in spite of the dreadful conditions in so much of education today, the imagination is being written about less now that it was two centuries ago. In fact, according to the Google research tool N-Gram Viewer, which tracks the frequency of word usage across decades, "imagination" is used less in published works now than in the year 1800. This is astounding when you consider how many more books and readers there are in the world today, especially on education! Narrow that down to the books on creativity and imagination in education, and the number of writers that have made substantial contributions to this topic becomes greatly conspicuous by their absence. So imagine my delight and level of engagement when I discovered the work of Maxine Greene and Paulo Freire and all they have to say about imagination, personal voice, and agency. These two scholars' lives and writing have so inspired me that I decided to learn everything I could from them and weave it together with my own perspective in an imaginary intellectual dialogue with the hope of discovering answers to the following questions.

The purpose of this book is to explore how imagination, which permeates every aspect of our life experience, helps develop personal and political awareness by enabling us to look beyond what is taken for granted, to question the normal, and to develop various ways of knowing, seeing, feeling, and acting upon positive social and educational changes in this current climate of accountability.

In addition to these questions, I ask: What role does imagination play in helping us develop awareness of personal perspective and identity in an era of standardization? And further, I inquire: How can we develop ways of imagining that will cultivate the opening of personal spaces of thought and expression beyond the status quo? How can the imagination be used to enhance both personal and communal ways of knowing, seeing, and being in the world?

Why I Chose an Imaginative Dialogue as a Theoretical Framework

For many years, I have entertained a personal fantasy of singing with the Everly Brothers. (Their harmonies strongly influenced the vocal duet styles of John Lennon and Paul McCartney as well as Paul Simon and Art Garfunkel.) When the Everly Brothers' songs come on the radio, I always join in and add a third part to their incredible blending of two distinct melodies that are joined in such a way that it is very difficult to tell which one is supposed to be the "counter melody." However, their singing invites other voices in the present while building on harmonic traditions that sound back to the origins of singing itself. This experience reminds me of what Oakeshott (1962) had to say about education as a historical conversation and about the framework of this book:

> As civilized human beings, we are the inheritors, neither of an inquiry about ourselves and the world, nor of an accumulating body of information, but of a conversation, begun in the primeval forests and extended and made more articulate in the course of centuries. It is a conversation which goes on both in public and *within each of ourselves*. (p. 490)

We can only vaguely speculate the immeasurable value that could be gained by listening in to preliterate conversations. However, a solid starting place within written accounts is provided by the conversations in Socratic dialogues. Plato's (n.d.) *Meno* is a good example of one of the clearer and more focused uses of this variety because it involves a shared definition and discussion of the question: "What is virtue?" I also found that Margaret Mead and James Baldwin used a dialogue format to discuss the specific topic called *A Rap on Race* (Baldwin & Mead, 1971). In this format, both are equals, yet they contribute different but complementary perspectives on the topic of race and society. During their discussion, they also draw from a wide range of sources as varied as Peter Ustinov to Allen Ginsberg to support their points of view (Baldwin & Mead, 1971).

Of course I am not the first to use imaginative dialogue in academic scholarship. The first book in this series by William Schubert (2009) gave voice to 426 "imaginary Utopians" that draw from a plethora interdisciplinary literature to elaborate and expand on Dewey's essay that appeared in the *New York Times* in 1933 that outlined Dewey's vision for utopian schools. In a related text on creativity and imagination, Willis and Schubert (1991) engage in dialogue. Also, Levitin (1982) created an "imaginary exchange of views" (p. 21-52) between Petrovsky, Jackobson, Toulmin, Vygotsky, Zinchenko, Schedrovitsky, Yaroshevsky, Cole, Davydov, Wertsch, Luria and Leontiev on Vygotskian perspectives of psychology. Japanese philosopher Daisaku Ikeda has published over 64 dialogues with a richly diverse group of people ranging from Makoto Nemoto (1978) to Elise Boulding (2010) to Mikhail Gorbachev (2005). By building on these examples of dialogue, as well as those that I will mention below, I frame an imaginary intellectual conversation between Maxine Greene and Paulo Freire, as they discuss the sociohistorical evolution of imagination.

My personal choice of these two voices emerges out of the role they have played in my own internalization of a curriculum of imagination. I was first introduced to Maxine Greene's work when I applied for doctoral studies. At that time, the selection of writing that each applicant had to read and reflect on for their writing sample was a chapter from *Releasing the Imagination* (Greene, 1995). From this introduction to doctoral studies and onward, her personal voice in writing and in actual speech became the voice of a muse in my head.

The first class I attended as a doctoral student was taught by William Reynolds. He introduced us to Paulo Freire's work not only with his words, but by the way the course was conducted. With Freire, I found a vocabulary for many aspects of my own personal and public practice of knowing and teaching. Together, their work epitomizes two aspects of imagination that are crucial to understanding what exactly is meant by this term when it is applied to the context of education. Their voices unite to express a holistic view of creative and critical applications of imagination. Louis Passmore (1975) sees the blending of both when he says:

> Critical thinking as it is exhibited in the great traditions conjoins imagination and criticism in a single form of thinking; in literature, science, history, philosophy or technology, the free flow of the imagination is controlled by criticism and criticisms are transformed into a new way of looking at things. Not that the free exercise of the imagination or raising of objections is in itself to be despised; the first can be suggestive of new ideas, the second can show the need for them. (p. 33)

Both Freire's and Greene's works contain a number of examples of dialogue in the form of intellectual conversation, so it is quite natural to build on this tradition. Weiss, Systra, and Slater (1998) composed an article out of a dinner conversation they had with Maxine Greene. Ayers (1995) also used this format in a conversation with Greene. In 1987 alone, Freire coauthored three "talking books" that were written in a dialogue format (Horton & Freire, 1990; Freire & Macedo, 1987; Shor & Freire, 1987).

So in this book, I am allowed to add my own voice and the voices of others to this imaginary duet. In my reflective commentary, I add Chatwin (1987) for his comments on imaginative "preliterate" practices of native Australians. I also quote from Gallas (2003) for her treatment of imagination as the connective power between schema and newly created thoughts. In my reflection on romantic imagination, I refer to Makdisi's (1998) treatment of the Colonial influence on the Romantic poets to confirm the transition from romantic to critical imagination. After Freire and Greene's exchange about emancipatory literacy, I refer to Moffett's concept of discourse (1968) as the *outward* expression of the holistic connection between personal meaning and external text. These citations provide a strong range of voices to contribute to the dialectical nature of the intellectual conversation and, as such, present a viable basis for a theoretical framework.

In the introduction to *The Landscape of Qualitative Research,* Denzin and Lincoln (2003), two of the most notable voices in qualitative research, share the metaphor of the qualitative researcher "as *bricoleur* or maker of quilts [who] uses aesthetic and material tools of his or her craft" (p. 6). This metaphor extends beyond the pragmatic to the "aesthetics of representation" into the concept of montage. This term is used in cinematography to describe the process of creating an aesthetic fusing together to form a newly created composite from footage shot in real time. The fusing together of film is often done in juxtaposition in ways to create greater depth and width to the representation of images. In a similar way, this work of imaginative dialogue as a framework for inquiry is a montage of quotes from Greene and Freire that are arranged to form a discursive interaction between the creative and critical aspects of imagination and blend my own voice in the dialogue.

While reading Greene and Freire's work and the leading theorists on literary, educational, social, critical, and psychological imagination and metaphor, I looked for emerging themes that were relevant to my quest for a curriculum of imagination. What I found served as a basis for the titles and subtitles of the chapters in this book. This imaginary dialogue continues throughout the text as a doorway and an extended framework into the content of each chapter that enabled me to move back and forth in the house of my inquiry without going to another structure.

Reviewing and Representing the Existing Literature on Imaginary Dialogue

An inquiry into imaginative curriculum with a boilerplate, book report approach to a review of the literature would be a contradiction of terms. By using a discourse of imaginative dialogue, I found that I was enabled to break out of a rut in the act of writing on one hand, while narrowing the range of leading voices down to the ones with whom I resonate the most on the other. This notion led me to thoroughly search the writing of Maxine Greene and Paulo Freire in order to find relevant passages from both that could be arranged in the format of an "intellectual conversation" without excessive conjecture. Moffett's (1968) concept of the discourse of conversation supports this notion: "Catechisms and imperatives, along with retorts, make the existential, rhetorical, and behavioural features of I-*you* most keenly felt" (p. 41). The use of dialogue accentuates the semantic aspects of the citations and puts them in more of a communicative form. The discourse of conversation adds to the personal meaning-making aspect of imagination by placing it in the context of the humanizing quality of exchanges between peers. By using this perspective, my hope is that future readers, especially my own students, will be provided with an overview of the concept of imagination and the epochs that formed the sociopolitical evolution of the term.

However, the dialogue is not limited to the work of Freire and Greene. As in any literature review, there are a number of quotes from others as well. Naturally, there are points in the imaginary dialogue where I constructed a composite expression of their voices and perspectives out of the tenor of all of their writing. The dialogue and my own perspective form another aspect of a montage that serves to synthesize and critique the quoted literature. This is accomplished by means of reflection and personal commentary interspersed throughout the dialogue, which also includes remarks on why I did or did not include specific passages from the review of literature.

The conversations are arranged in a way that explores the sociopolitical evolution of the definition of imagination that exists in the prevailing paradigms of philosophy and science. These paradigms may have had a historical beginning at a certain period, but my review suggests that the cultural conditions created by changes in thought are still very much present in the 21st century.

Writing as Imaginative Inquiry

The act of writing is itself a "method of inquiry, a way of finding out about yourself and your topic" (Richardson, 2003, p. 499). Through writing the inner landscape of thought is merged with personalized communication. And yet the field of educational inquiry is still strongly influenced by 19th century forms of static writing. Richardson views the field of qualitative research as limited because writers are expected to "silence their own voices and to view themselves as contaminants" (p. 501) and further that the "writing up" of educational research "validates a mechanistic model of writing, shutting down the creativity and sensibilities of the individual writer/researcher" (p. 502).

Conversely, it is through imaginative engagement of personal sensibilities, where the divide between the objective and subjective aspects is transcended, that learning is most likely to occur.

Writing as inquiry provides me with a lens for viewing a curriculum of imagination at work in a number of ways. First of all, the connection between imagination, personal meaning, and metaphor was made very real to me through my desire to clearly represent the nature of standardization as a wall, imagination as both a mirror and a lamp, and the soil of Romanticism itself. These are a few of the examples of metaphor that helped me understand and express the content of this inquiry. Secondly, through the process of seeking a way to write about imagination in a way that made sense to me, as well as my audience, I began to see that the act of writing is not only the source of my inquiry, it is also the goal. That is, I began to see that a curriculum of imagination can be discovered and practiced through the act of writing in the language of imagination, which is personal metaphor, which unites inner landscapes with forms of discourse (Moffett, 1968). Thirdly, in expanding Moffett's notion of "learning to write by writing" (pp. 188-210) to the level of writing this book, I saw the immense value of seeking "feedback" (Moffett, 1968, p. 188). Consequently, I have literally written, received feedback, and revised the contents of this book a number of times and have continued to learn more with every new draft of the text. In his elaboration about the writing, feedback, and revision process, Moffett goes on to say:

> The fact that one writes by oneself does not at all diminish the need for response, since one writes for others. Even when one purports to be writing for oneself, for pure self-expression, if there is such a thing—one cannot escape the ultimately social implications inherent in any use of language. (p. 191)

The act of writing itself is educative through the formation of personalized meaning creation when students explore their own experience with the content of inquiry. Maxine Greene (1995) places writing at the center of the learning experience when she says that "by writing that I often manage to name alternatives and to open myself to possibilities. This is what I think learning ought to be" (p. 107). Writing is a form of thinking and an extension of the reading process, and there are no limits to how it can be used as a medium for learning across every content area.

By intertwining theory and personal story, I found a continual unity in using imagination and metaphor in the process of writing about these topics. In fact, after I centered my study in the imagination, I found a natural progression in the ordering of the chapters. This was not so much a linear configuration as it was a multilayered inquiry into the implications of contrasting the freedom of the imaginative and aesthetic realm with the cultural effects of standardization. This is accomplished through authorship of imaginative dialogue constructed, for the most part, of actual quotations in each chapter and personal narrative. I close this section referring again to the perspective of one of the leading voices in the field of qualitative research.

Richardson (2003) sees the positive impact that feminist researchers brought to bear: In making "the personal the political, the personal is the grounding for theory" (p. 506). In the development of my research on the imagination, I came to the conclusion that the strongest way I had of presenting my inquiry was to view myself as the subject. This is done through reflective and reflexive applications to the both the theory and the practice of imaginative education while maintaining an autobiographical perspective.

Most of the books on imagination have been written by scholars from the fields of psychology, literature, or philosophy. As important as imagination is to learning, the field of education is disproportionately underrepresented in this topic. There have been many books written on creativity and a growing number on the critical pedagogy. This book is written as an inquiry into ways that imagination brings *both these perspectives together* in past, present, and future, and personal and shared meaning making. It is my hope that this book will be read by those who are weary of scripted "knowledge" and the sense of being "walled in" by the present obsession with standards and "norms." Those within this group include concerned parents, citizens, and policymakers; students of education from all levels; and most of all teachers, who should be on the vanguard of social change but are often consigned to the role of "clerks of the empire" (Giroux, 1988, p. 91) through standardized practices and accountability requirements that leave little room for creative expression while weighing the teacher down with "accountability" paperwork and logistical procedure. All of these elements together create obstacles or walls for both teachers and students.

Wall Metaphor

For most of my life, I have been fascinated with the notion of transcending various kinds of walls. One of my favorite movies as a child was *The Great Escape* (Sturges, 1963), which was based on the true story of an elaborate plan by Allied Forces officers to escape from a Nazi prisoner of war camp. Another more recent favorite movie is *The Fugitive* (Kopelson & Davis, 1993), also based on a true story of an innocent man who was falsely accused of murdering his wife. In both cases, the theme of breaking out of confinement in the cause of social justice is clearly stated. In *The Great Escape*, the prisoners had no way of knowing just how long the war would continue, and many of the prisoners were murdered in cold blood, in violation of the Geneva Convention rules of engagement. In *The Fugitive*, the protagonist is framed by agents of a pharmaceutical company because he is privy to an elaborate scheme to cover their tracks in the production and distribution of a horribly defective prescription medicine. The relevance of these references is deeply personal, but that is where metaphoric connections originate. Another example comes from my own experience.

When I was a small-for-my-age 11-year-old, much to my own surprise, I hit a baseball over the fence in a little league game. At the time, I had no way of comprehending the impact that event would have in shaping my inner landscape. From then on, I have literally dreamed hundreds of times of hitting a baseball over the wall in a major league park. Since I began my doctoral studies, this dream has occurred more frequently and has become a very personal metaphor for triumph in spite of both inward and outward walls.

In a more universal sense, walls are metaphoric of standardization, limitation, and control. In the chapters that follow, I use the wall metaphor to describe excellence and accountability, which, in reality, are just buzzwords for contrived and homogeneous educational methodology. The current obsession with these concepts has served to create a vast market of "wall-building" textbook and test preparation materials.

I also use the wall metaphor to think about the ways that essentialism and racial and ethnic labeling prevent us from understanding and relating to the "other." The role of personal story in creating empathy is presented as a means of moving beyond walls of this kind. In addition, the wall metaphor provided me with a way to describe the well-guarded borders between content area subjects and between "academic" and "vocational" tracking practices.

While I do remain hopeful that wholesale changes can occur in the present system of North American education, at the same time, I acknowledge that the deep-seated desire in man to uphold unjust networks of power will likely serve to keep walls intact. In spite of this, the creative power of the imagination is able to lift both teachers and students above walls and into a boundless personal and communal quest for unscripted ways of knowing and being. In an interview with Bill Ayers, Maxine Greene (1995) offered this insight into what keeps her reaching beyond confinement:

> I know that the real joy in life stems from the feeling of incompletion, of not having found the way, so, like so many others; I reach out for roles to play, for personalities to come in touch with, for an abundance of desire. I do not want to end up in isolation, even in the midst of things; I never want to become accustomed to a dry little life. And I realize fully that to live otherwise is up to me. (p. 323)

I had already finished most of the first draft of this inquiry when I began reading Greene's *Dialectic of Freedom* (1988). I was grateful to discover that she had written about metaphoric walls so extensively in this book. For her, a wall is a metaphor that describes barriers to personal meaning and agency that must be "named" before we can move beyond them. Some of these are listed as "limitations on free speech, mindlessness. mechanism, routine behaviors, the rule of 'brute' habit—none of which would be noticed by those who were somnolent or who had no wish to move beyond" (Greene, 1988, p. 6). To Greene, freedom is the absence of controlled meaning; in "open contexts where persons attend to one another with interest, regard, and care, there is the place for the appearance of freedom" (Greene, 1988, p. xi). It is my hope that the field of education in particular will be awakened to name and move beyond the walls that confine teachers, students, and school leaders in unjust, mediocre, and dehumanizing stasis.

A Panoramic View of the Chapters

This book consists of a prologue, six chapters, and an epilogue. Except for the section of dialogue as literature review in Chapter 1, each chapter describes some aspect of walls in the present system of education and suggests ways that imagination can transcend these limitations through the world-creating power of personal metaphor. This inquiry into a curriculum of imagination describes the role of verbal, emotional, visual, somatic, and musical literacies that supersede walls between specific content areas as well as group labels and cultural identities. A dialogue between Maxine Greene and Paulo Freire serves as an ongoing literature review and theoretical framework for each chapter.

In this Prologue, I have provided a sociohistorical context through sharing how my personal history has instilled a passion to understand imagination. I have also briefly discussed the current landscape of education. This is followed by the focus of this inquiry and an introduction to the concept of an imaginative dialogue. I close the prologue by discussing how the act of writing creates personal meaning as well as how "wall" metaphor came into being.

Chapter 1, "What Is Imagination?," is an intellectual dialogue between Maxine Greene and Paulo Freire, with my own commentary interspersed at various points in the conversation. While this is an imaginary dialogue, it is based, for the most part, on actual quotes from two of the most notable voices in educational theory and practice in the last 40 years. For the sake of conversational representation, I provide a minimal amount of editorial content that is based on a composite expression of Greene's and Freire's philosophical voices and writing styles. This conversation is predicated upon a form of dialectic inquiry that dates back to Ancient Greece. The dialogue provides an overview of the sociohistorical evolution of the concept of imagination from the existential perspective of both participants.

In Chapter 2, "Walls of Standardization," I discuss the history of trends in standardized testing and curriculum in the United States during the 20th century. This includes a brief description of "dark imagination" (Greene, personal communication, 6/14/06) at work through the genesis of intelligence testing and the role it has played in the eugenics movement and, later, in student tracking and labeling. The dehumanizing effects of Freire's notion of the "banking method" of education and Greene's concept of "seeing things small" serve as a context for this discussion.

In Chapter 3, "Metaphor: The Language of Imagination," I focus on the role of metaphor and the imagination in opening spaces for personal discovery, construction of meaning, and the creation of personal agency. After introducing the topic with a continuation of Greene and Freire's dialogue, I discuss the centrality of metaphor in both the conscious and subconscious levels of thinking. This experience is not limited to the cognitive domain; it also includes the physical and the emotional domains in perceiving, interpreting, and expressing meaning.

In Chapter 4, "Sensing Gaps," I discuss the role of critical imagination in perceiving the unanswered, the unfinished, and the unjust that moves us beyond the taken-for-granted and the status quo. This capacity has suffered enormous setbacks in the present system of "official knowledge" (Apple, 1993) and highly contrived practices of classroom accountability, and yet the capacity of problem finding is central to personal discovery, political awareness, and social change. Henle (1986) discusses four sources of "sensing gaps." I build on her work with salient examples of application of each of these. This leads to a discussion of an "incubation period" in moving beyond the given. I conclude Chapter 4 by suggesting ways that nonverbal metaphor creates creative and critical expression.

In Chapter 5, "Toward Empathic Imagination," I discuss ways that social imagination is vital to understanding the "other." Because "no man is an island" (Donne, 1839, pp. 574–575), a curriculum of imagination must also focus on the horizontal as it enables students to understand and relate from their own unique vantage points and personal identities. North America is no longer solely comprised of a homogeneous culture of Northern European heritage. In order to inspire students to participate in democracy in this century, they must learn to value dialogue with those who are different. This involves far more than having an attitude of "tolerance" or "seeing no colors." Suggestions for using literature, and music to enhance empathy and understanding are considered.

In Chapter 6, "A Curriculum of Imagination in the Making," I present a brief review of the main topics in each chapter, followed by a view of a curriculum of imagination in the making. This is accomplished by connecting my inquiry to Schwab's notion of the four commonplaces of curriculum: milieus, teacher, subject matter, and learner. I finish the chapter by presenting connections between democracy in the making and a curriculum of imagination in the making.

In the Epilogue, I discuss a number of doors of inquiry that have opened to me as a result of writing this book and the tensions that have emerged in my own teaching and research over the last several years. These include both theoretical and practical applications of the ideas in this inquiry and a preview of landscapes that beckon me into further exploration.

1

What is Imagination?

An Imaginary Intellectiual Dialogue Between Maxine Greene and Paulo Freire

A literature review and a Platonic dialogue both begin with an exploratory question that often begins with a definition followed by supporting citations from several authors. Here I start with Freire's question and Greene's response, followed by quotes from Dewey (1934), Shaull (2003), and Gallas (2003), in support of a personal view of the definition of imagination.

Paulo: You refer to imagination quite often in your writing, and that is a very broad term. What is your personal understanding of its meaning?

Maxine: I'm glad you emphasized the word "personal" because that is the modus operandi of imagination. Indeed, "out of all our cognitive capacities, imagination is the one that . . . allows us to break with the taken for granted, to set aside familiar distinctions and definitions" (Greene, 1995, p. 3) and break with what is suppos-

A Curriculum of Imagination in an Era of Standardization, pages 1–13
Copyright © 2013 by Information Age Publishing
All rights of reproduction in any form reserved.

edly fixed and finished (p. 19). This must be why Dewey (1934) described this capacity as a gateway through which meanings derived from past experiences find their way into the present in what he calls the "the conscious adjustment of the new and the old." (p. 272). On the same page he goes on to say that imagination more than any other capacity "breaks through the inertia of habit," while it allows us to "glimpse what might be and what is not yet" (Greene, 1995, p. 19).

Paulo: I see imagination as a humanizing capacity that enables us to act upon and transform our world through the first-hand discovery and naming of our own worlds of meaning. This is what my friend Richard Shaull (2003) had in mind when he said that:

> [this] *world* to which he relates is not a static and closed order, a *given* reality which man must accept and to which he must adjust; rather, it is a problem to be worked on and solved. It is the material used by man to create history, a task which he performs as he overcomes that which is dehumanizing at any particular time and place and dares to create qualitatively new. (p. 32)

I really appreciate the emphasis in both these statements on the personal meaning-making capacity of imagination as well as the emphasis on action. It reminds me of Dewey's notion that "mind is primarily a verb" and therefore involves the whole being. Imagination integrates the cognitive, the emotional, and the physical by connecting concepts or images with our experience in comprehension and personal meaning-making. This process involves more than the ability to "reflect" and recapture images. Imagination enables us to perceive, uniquely interpret, and express in a new way. Karen Gallas (2003) clearly articulates this by saying:

> [Imagination] is both mundane and transcendent. It reflects our experiences back to us in recognizable forms and images that do not surprise or alarm us, but it also creates unique representations of that same experience whose form and image suggest that our experience has dimensions beyond those we have perceived. (pp. 37–38)

Imagination and Hope

One of the ways that imagination helps to create personal agency and political awareness is by enabling the imaginer to resist the present order and see beyond obstacles. Innovation in any domain, including science, literature, and sociopolitical change, all begin with imagination and hope.

Maxine: In this present climate of stasis and predefinition, we couldn't have picked a more opportune time to discuss these matters, but one reason that I think we get along so well, Paulo, is that we have never ceased to exercise the kind of "thinking that refuses mere compliance, that looks down roads not yet taken to the shape of a more fulfilling social order, to more vibrant ways of being in the world" (Greene, 1995, p. 5).

Paulo: I agree! Any "attempt to do without hope, in the struggle to improve the world, as if that struggle could be reduced to calculated acts alone, or a purely scientific approach, is a frivolous illusion" (Freire, 1992, p. 8). I would even go so far as to say that "there is no change without a dream, as there is no dream without hope.... I see history as opportunity and not determinism" (p. 91).

Maxine: That is right! We can refuse fatalism and move beyond "things as they are," as Stevens expresses in one of my favorite poems, *The Man with Blue Guitar*. The "blue guitar became a metaphor for the imagination" (Greene, 2001, p. 91). Two of my favorite verses may help set the stage for further dialogue.

> They said, "You have a blue guitar,
> You do not play things as they are.'
>
> The man replied, "Things as they are
> Are changed upon the blue guitar."
>
> And they said then, "But play, you must,
> A tune beyond us, yet ourselves,
>
> A tune upon the blue guitar
> Of things exactly as they are."
>
> Throw away the lights, the definitions,
> And say of what you see in the dark
>
> That it is this or that it is that,
> But do not use the rotted names.
>
> (Stevens, 1954, pp. 165–183)

Using "rotted names" (Stevens, p. 183) is the result of the lack of both creative and critical perspectives of imagination. In this way, my notion of imaginative aesthetic awakenings and your work in critical consciousness are one. I know I resound with all your work when I say that imagination enables students to "look through their own eyes, to find their own voices to avoid the formulations devised by official others" (Greene, 1995, p. 20).

There is a connection between "rotted names" for things and the loss of hope. When students are encouraged in first-hand inquiry and free to use their own personal metaphors for experience, the hope of discovering yet more emerges. When students can "own" their inquiry, when it becomes part of their identity, personal vision and motivation increase!

Paulo: I have no trouble understanding the imagination in those terms! The banking concept of education creates the very opposite of hope because it carries "the assumption of a dichotomy between man and the world: man is merely in the world, not with the world or with others; man is spectator, not re-creator. In this view, man is not a conscious being (corpo consciente); He is rather the possessor of a consciousness: an empty "mind passively open to the reception of deposits of reality from the world outside" (Freire, 1970, p. 75). Imagination enables both reflection and creative generation. That is the very wellspring of hope!

Imagination as a Mirror

The reflective aspect of imagination is a precursor to personal interpretation and creation. Reflective imagination attends to forms and abilities that are often equated as a general definition of intelligence. It is the ability to comprehend, reproduce, and perform any task ranging from open heart surgery to comprehensible first or second language fluency, number sentences to the construction of a residential septic system. When this type of imagination is at work, people are liable to say, "She really captured the essence of that," or "He did an amazing job on this." Frequently, people start with this aspect of imagination and learn all they can from others before they move on to generative imagination. Bob Dylan's work as a singer/songwriter is a good example of this. In his early work, Dylan sought to emulate Woody Guthrie's writing and singing style, and even his dress. In just a few years, his genius as one of the most original songwriters in history became evident. Imagination is reflective, but it is also so much more.

Maxine: That is a very present tense view of imagination, Paulo! When we consider the sociohistorical evolution of imagination, one salient feature to consider is that, for the most part, imagination was not considered generative until the Romantic era. Up to that time, it was treated as fanciful to the Greeks or even a source of demonic peril in the Dark Ages. After that came the "Enlightenment," which brought in a strong emphasis on the rational and "pure" scientific objectivity, which later became the foundation for the present obsession with standardization. The ancient and medieval models share similar views of imagination. In both periods, it was treated as a distraction to reality that was at best "reproductive of sensuous impressions or conveying conceptions to the senses, never properly as a productive autonomous activity" (Croce, 1972, p. 170). Consequently, originality only moved in a "downward" direction. This reminds me of Dewey's (1934) comments on the metaphysical split that characterized the Platonic world.

> Plato's ladder is, moreover, a one-way ascent; there is no return from the highest beauty to perceptual experience.... Sense [perception] seems...to Plato, to be a seduction that leads man away from the spiritual. It is tolerated only as a vehicle [intermediary] through which man may be brought to an intuition of immaterial and nonsensuous essence. (pp. 291–293)

Not much changed in this regard in the medieval period. Both Aquinas and Augustine viewed the material world as a distraction and the field of imagination as a threat to "pure" contemplation. In fact, Kieran Egan (1992) goes so far as to say that Aquinas viewed imagination as a "particularly weak part of the mind, susceptible to confusing its images with reality" (p. 17).

No wonder there was so little innovation in the Western world during these periods! With such a sharp distinction between the material and the spiritual world and the strong emphasis on the dichotomy between body and mind, a paradigm of superstitious fear acted as a shroud to discovery. It is hard to believe that as late as the 17th century, two of Copernicus's followers were persecuted for their view of a heliocentric solar system. In 1600, Bruno was burned at the stake in Rome for his view of a universe without walls, and in 1635, Galileo was forced to recant the view that the Earth revolved around the Sun, or he too would have been killed!

Preliterate Imagination

In many cases "preliterate" imagination is also precolonial and, therefore, has strong implications in terms of creating personal and political awareness. It certainly needs to be considered in any discussion of post-Colonialism.

Paulo: Before we go any further, we should talk about the "preliterate" era. There are still many of the so called "indigenous populations" that have been "reading the world" with imagination in a highly creative system of problem solving and oral tradition.

Preliterate cultures were held together through fantastic stories, songs, and images, and poems and dances (Egan, 1992, p. 11). This aspect of the imagination proved to be effective enough to sustain the culture of some tribes even in "modern" times. Chatwin (1987) reports that when the native Australians cross the vast wilderness of the Outback on foot, they use singing maps passed down from their ancestors. Their songs describe what land features to look for in this barren setting, which has few trees or other landmarks. Singing not only helps them to remember, but soothes their fear of the unknown. This is an aspect of literacy that we need to learn from them. It has certainly played a strongly defining role in my life as both a student and a teacher. Music has helped me to stay on track!

Paulo: I constantly think of my own people in South America. These populations were in place before the White population arrived. Thus, the White population became involved with an established civilization that also had its own voice or voices. These populations have the right to the voices that were silenced by the Hispanic–Portuguese invasion (Freire, 1987, p. 57). In all my literacy work in Brazil and other places, I have drawn on the voices of the people that were already fluent in reading the world to enable them to read the word both creatively and critically. I have drawn upon their culture of work and storytelling as well as their music and dance to help them make connections between experience and further discovery.

Maxine: I am glad you mentioned dancing because it is in itself a language that is rich in the metaphor of movement. The present emphasis on technology may serve to devolve a culture from this kind of richness of expression. "I always want to recommend a session of dancing before the young people take to their computers—even as I want to enable young people to try to express through movement sometimes how they feel, what they desire, what they understand" (Greene, 2001, pp. 95–96).

Generative Imagination

This juncture in the sociohistorical evolution of imagination is vital to the creation of personal voice. In this paradigm, the dehumanizing effects of the religious empire began to be shed, creating space for the expression of emotion and the world creating power of metaphor.

Paulo: With an emphasis on feeling and desire, we have really come to the Romantic period. How has your personal experience shaped your view of this era in the evolution of imagination?

Maxine: I can personally resonate with some of the voices in the Romantic era because like them, my emphasis on the poetic and the use of metaphor in literature created misunderstanding with those who have sought to departmentalize and fragment the field of philosophy. I was demeaned in my early days of college teaching by being told I was too "literary" to do philosophy. That seemed to mean that they thought I was ill-equipped to do the sort of detached and rigorous analysis of language games that for a long time dominated the academic world (Greene, 1995, p. 113).

One place I found refuge was in the work of the romantic poets. Blake and Wordsworth in particular meant a lot to me because they embody a "resistance to predefined norms and systems—whether embodied in the artificial order of the city or the neo-classical rules of poetry" (Greene, 1988, p. 29).

Paulo: Now you are speaking my language! The praxis of domination operates by superimposing its own language and denying the oppressed "the right to say their own words and think their own thoughts" (Freire, 1970, p. 126). The Romantics increased an awareness of the value of liberating individuals from having to think, speak, and act out of an unnatural self.

Maxine: Yes! The Romantic Movement released the individual to "find his own voice, to express in 'common language of men' what he himself thought and felt... to a world into which an imaginative person can release value, a world which 'we half create what we perceive,' as Wordsworth said" (Greene, 1988, p. 29).

Paulo: So we are indebted to the Romantic poets when we speak of the power to synthesize experience into newly generated meaning.

Maxine: Right, Paulo! And that reminds me of something that Mary Warnock (1976) had to say about this:

> Presumably the simple rehearsal of mental images, reproducing in representations what we have already acquired in perception, would not count as the work of the poetic imagination, and would be ascribed to memory alone. Imagination has to do more. It must try to create one thing (one thought or form) out of the many different elements of experience; and this entails extracting the essence of the differing phenomena of experience. (p. 2)

She goes on to say that "Coleridge derived the thought that poetic imagination must be able to bring together, as Schelling says, even contradictories" (p. 92). Imagination creates new orders as it brings these "severed parts together" (Woolf, 1976, p. 72). The Romantic notion of the poetic was an evolutionary advance in this direction, and yet I am aware that our conversation is still incomplete.

Critical Imagination

Like choking weeds in an exotic garden of wonderfully unique and vibrant expression, ethnocentric modernization and Colonialism grew up in the same post-Enlightenment soil as the Romantic poets (Makdisi, 1998, presents a thorough treatment of this notion). Critical imagination is essential to the process of naming walls and actively moving out of the marginal and subaltern and into personal and political freedom.

> **Paulo:** In that context, the Romantic Movement was a good start; however, it is not enough to make problematic class conflict, gender, or racial inequalities. Furthermore, the romantic model completely ignores the cultural capital of subordinate groups and assumes that all people have the same access to reading or that reading is part of the cultural capital of all people. This failure to address questions of cultural capital or various structural inequalities means that the romantic model tends to reproduce the cultural capital of the dominant class. (Freire & Macedo, 1987, p. 149)
>
> Critical imagination enables students to "interrogate and selectively appropriate those aspects of the dominant culture that will provide them with the basis for defining and transforming, rather than merely serving, the wider social order" (Arnowitz , in Freire & Macedo, 1987, p. 152).

This is a very important aspect for the reason for emphasizing imaginative curriculum in both the creative and critical dimensions. Within the creative aspect lies the ability to make personal metaphoric connections to content. Out of the critical dimension, students are enabled to uncover whose interests are being served by the sociohistorical content of knowledge that is "taught."

> **Maxine:** Yes, it takes both creative and critical imagination to personally define and actively transform. Without both these aspects, "personal agency" is just another "rotted name."

The most effective way of teaching critical imagination is to continually present what is reliable and legitimate. When the United States Department of the Treasury (2003) released the new versions of paper currency, they also undertook a campaign to prevent counterfeiting by displaying the unique features of genuine currency on posters in many different languages.

This serves as a metaphor for critical imagination in formation. In other words, the most effective way to enhance critical consciousness, as Freire calls it, and wide awakeness, to use Greene's terminology, is through interaction with reality. In Freire's case, the very fact that he cared enough to go to the farmers in Brazil and demonstrate critical pedagogy, drawing on the language and "preliterate" culture and understanding that the natives already possessed, provided a contrast in bold relief to the banking model of education. His obvious compassion and lack of patronization expressed a sample of reality that exposed dehumanization and exploitation through unjust power relations much more fully by his actions than his words.

In Greene's case, she expresses wide-awakeness through her passion for personal meaning that she finds in so many areas of dance, film, literature, philosophy, and the arts. In support of her notion of wide-awakeness, she draws on Dewey's (1934) perspective that the opposite of aesthetic education is anesthetic. It is her passion for meaning and her example of continual quest, even in her nineties, that provide us with a sample of the real, which exposes so many practices of one-dimensional meaning and having the final official word.

A clear example of critical imagination in formation is found in Gaughan's book for secondary language arts teachers called *Cultural Reflections* (1997). In one of his exercises with his students, he quotes from Orwell in *Animal Farm* (1946) and has the students compare Squealer's speech to one of Ronald Reagan's 1984 campaign speeches (Gaughan, 1997, p.101). This was quite interesting, but as I was reading this work, I immediately applied it to the rhetoric of fear that has so characterized post 9/11 White

House speech writing. In this context, Squealer's words seem more apt to-day than they did in the height of the Cold War. "Bravery is not enough," said Squealer. "Loyalty and obedience are more important.... One false step and our enemies would be back on us. Surely comrades, you do not want Jones back" (Orwell, 1946, p. 60).

Cartesian Influence in the Cognitive Model

In some ways, cognitive psychology is a return to Descartes' notion of reducing mental processes to value-neutral mathematical functioning. I include this section because it expresses the dialectic nature of the socio-historical development of imagination in its view of the computational model of intelligence. At the same time, in a more nuanced consideration, the cognitive model is responsible for turning behaviorism on its head.

> **Paulo:** Even the cognitive problem solving model of learning falls short of drawing on the student's life experience, language, and culture. In this model, reading is seen as an intellectual process designed to take students "through a series of fixed, value free and universal stages of development" (Walmsey, 1981, p. 82). This emphasis on increasing levels of complexity leaves little room for "thorough critical reflection, regarding [the students] own practical experience and the ends that motivate them in order, in the end, to organize the findings and thus replace mere opinion about facts with an increasingly rigorous understanding of their significance" (Freire, 1987, p. 148).

> **Maxine:** That is true! Personal awakening to meaning does not occur on some kind of timeline. The movement of life itself is multilayered, and it flows in many directions. Certainly the field of cognitive psychology brought some needed changes in the way the imagination is viewed. Chomsky and colleagues posited a theory that humans possess an innate faculty for acquiring languages. This capacity is generative and therefore accounts for the ability to create newly formed sentences. This view, on one hand, confirms the Romantics' view of imagination as a generative instead of an imitative medium. On the other hand, our minds are so much *more* than chemical computers! Out of the wholeness of body, mind, and emotions, imagination releases passion, wonder, pain, empathy, and a sense of incompleteness leading to personal discovery.

One can easily see the limitations that the computational model of the brain would have on the realm of the imagination. No matter how much "memory" a computer has, it is incapable of being a source of emotional knowing, empathy, and personal agency. While allowing at least the value of image and advancing the concept of the human ability to generate ideas, cognitive psychology falls short of giving a full account of the potential of the imagination.

> **Paulo:** I agree, of course, but we must not forget about the role that Chomsky's work played in critically challenging behaviorism. The cognitive framework at least allows people to be human! Imagination is useless to behaviorism because it reduces humanity to the level of the ahistorical animal, unable to take on life, and "because they do not take it on, they cannot construct it; and if they do not construct it, they cannot transform its configuration" (Freire, 1970, p. 98).

> **Maxine:** Yes! Those who are only concerned with behavioral outcomes have little interest in the inner landscape of a person's imagination. The main focus, instead, is on that which is quantifiable in "norm referenced" comparisons. Tragically, this psychological notion tends to act as a wall to the opening of new ways of "looking at things [that are] wholly at odds with the technicist and behaviorist emphases we still find in American schools" (Greene, 1988, p. 126).

To be human is so much more than these two concepts of mind as computer or the behaviorist notion of humans as animalistic. Of course, neither one of these theories can be completely ignored. We know, for example, that the computer metaphor certainly fits some aspects of memory. I also acknowledge the role that behaviorism plays when humans act like animals—in serial murders, for example. At the same time, the expression of imagination through all the somatic, emotional, and mental capacities may very well define what it means to be human.

The Praxis of Emancipatory Literacy

This section is central to all that follows in this inquiry. It expresses the role of imagination in joining the personal and the universal, the subjective and the objective, the private and the public. Having accomplished this, imagination enables the expression of these connections through what James Moffett calls the "universe of discourse" (1968).

Paulo: Excellent point! However, it must be emphasized: Praxis requires more than new ways of looking at things. Once we break with the taken-for-granted, there must also be *reflection and action* that remove the separation between ourselves and "the other." I always have something to learn from others. "I engage in dialogue because I recognize the social and not merely the individualistic character of the process of knowing" (Freire & Macedo, 1995, p. 179).

Maxine: Exactly! Even when we are alone, imagination enables us to enter into a "dialogue" with text. This is where creative and critical imagination work together to create openings in praxis. Through imagination, we are enabled to bring the "severed parts" of our own personal perspective and that which is expressed in the text. At the same time, the critical aspect of imagination enables us to question, to wonder, and to sense the incompleteness in the way others interpret things. This "approach challenges subject–object separations" (Greene, 1995, p. 99) and breaks with the "hegemony of language over perception and conceptualization of reality" (Bakhtin, 1981, p. 369).

Paulo: That really brings us to the essence of what it means to educate. When the role of imagination is placed in the context of the praxis of emancipatory literacy, it expresses itself in:

> a creative act that involves a critical comprehension of reality. The knowledge of earlier knowledge, gained by the learners as a result of analyzing praxis in its social context, opens to them the possibility of a new knowledge. The new knowledge reveals the reason for being that is behind the facts, thus demythologizing the false interpretations of these same facts. Thus there is no longer any separation between thought-language and objective reality. The reading of a text now demands a reading within the social context to which it refers. (Freire, 1987, p. 157)

This statement does indeed put imagination at the very center of learning by making salient the creative process that is needed to personalize meaning. Imagination creates synthesis between a student's internal perspective and the world as text. Once these connections are made, they can be transformed into an infinite variety of personal expression. Writing is essentially the act of generative thinking. The same is true of music composition, interpretive dance, works of art, and every known variety of craftsmanship.

Maxine: Imagination may be responsible for the very texture of our experience. "Once we do away with habitual separations of the subjective from the objective, the inside from the outside, appearances from reality, we might be able to give imagination its proper importance and grasp what it means to place imagination at the core of understanding" (Greene, 1995, p. 141).

2

Walls of Standardization

Two of the most fitting metaphors for the effects of standardization on schooling are seen in the writings of Maxine Greene and Paulo Freire. Greene's (1995) notion of "seeing things small" and Freire's (1970) concept of the "banking model of education" are both incomparable ideas that must be included in any discussion of imaginative education. My fictional dialogue continues with a discussion of these metaphors.

Banking Education and Seeing Things Small

Maxine: One of the clearest illustrations of the absence of imagination in schooling is found in your notion of the banking model of education.

Paulo: Your work that describes "seeing things small" addresses many of the same issues out of your unique perspective.

Maxine: Let's look at both together. The phrase "seeing things small" comes from a novel by Thomas Mann (1955). In it, he says that

A Curriculum of Imagination in an Era of Standardization, pages 15–28
Copyright © 2013 by Information Age Publishing
All rights of reproduction in any form reserved.

leaders and generals have to be able to view things small in order to deal with "the lives and deaths of so many living beings" (pp. 12–13). Seeing things small means to look from a "detached point of view and to be concerned with trends and tendencies rather than the intentionality and concreteness of everyday life" (1995, p. 10).

Paulo: In seeing things small, students are viewed as objects and passive containers waiting to be filled with the daily quota of "knowledge" and then tested and classified by statistical means. The banking method of education operates by "receiving, filing, and storing the deposits. They do, it is true, have the opportunity to become collectors or cataloguers of the things they store. But in the last analysis, it is men themselves who are filed away through the lack of creativity, transformation, and knowledge" (Freire, 1970, p. 72).

Maxine: "Seeing things small looks at schooling through the lenses of a system, a vantage point of power or existing ideologies—taking a primarily technical point of view" (Greene, 1995, p. 11).

Paulo: The oppressors have to maintain that vantage point in order to preserve their interests. Imaginative education is a threat to that perspective. Therefore, it is not surprising that the banking concept of education regards men as adaptable, manageable beings. The more students work at storing the deposits entrusted to them, the less they develop the critical consciousness that would result from their intervention in the world as transformers of that world. The more completely they accept the passive role imposed on them, the more they tend simply to adapt to the world as it is and the fragmented view of reality deposited in them. The capability of banking education to minimize or annul the students' creative power and to stimulate their credulity serves the interests of the oppressors, who care neither to have the world revealed nor to see it transformed. The oppressors use their "humanitarianism" to preserve a profitable situation. Thus they react almost instinctively against any experiment in education that stimulates the critical faculties and is not content with a partial view of reality but always seeks out the ties that link one point to another and one problem to another. Indeed, the interests of the oppressors lie in "changing the consciousness of the oppressed, not the situation which oppresses them," for the more the oppressed can be led to that situation, the more easily they can be dominated (Freire, 1970, pp. 73–74).

Maxine: So the notion of schooling "behind walls" serves the interest of those in power, by maintaining control through smallness and abstraction and detachment and fragmentation of school subjects from the context of real life.

Paulo: That's right! And detachment from real life prevents students from taking ownership of their own learning. This has been a problem for at least as long as the Colonial period, but it really became salient during the 20th century and continues today under different names.

Standardization is a 20th century concept that has increased its influence on our culture up to the present time. This is certainly the case in the field of education. Freire and Greene's concepts of smallness, abstraction, and decontextualized, fragmented "knowledge" delivered in the "banking method" are just as relevant now as they were 20 to 35 years ago.

In a culture that worships the "bottom line," statistical comparisons, and measurement, there is much more of a tendency to deceptively report quantitatively expressed "progress" than to make substantial changes. In the world of business, for example, thousands of jobs have been eliminated in order to make annual business reports look better to stockholders. The trouble with this reasoning is that sooner or later real conditions come to the surface and the use of window dressing and manipulation of statistics can no longer hide the reality of failure. Throughout this chapter, I will focus on the history of standardization and the how and why of its growth and influence on the field of education. Context is everything. It is crucial to understand the origin and nature of the walls before we can rise above them.

Dark Imagination and the History of Standardization

In a telephone conversation with Maxine Greene (personal communication, 6/14, 2006), she stressed the need to include a section in my book on the dark side of imagination. As an example of this, she specifically mentioned Hitler's "final solution," which is, of course, a euphemistic expression for the Third Reich's attempt at eliminating the Jewish "race." I found her suggestions to be very compelling since I had already planned on including a section about the history of intelligence testing and the eugenics movement. My literature search brought me to Black's (2003) *War Against the Weak: Eugenics and America's Campaign to Create a Master Race*. This book documents the connection between the American eugenics movement and Nazi Germany. The stated purpose of this movement was to "immediately sterilize fourteen million people in the United States and millions more worldwide—the 'lower tenth'—and then continuously eradicate the remaining lowest tenth until only a pure Nordic super race remained. Ultimately, some 60,000 Americans were coercively sterilized and the total is probably much higher" (Black, 2003, p. xvi).

It is remarkable to consider the extent of the influence that the concept of the biological superiority of the White race held in shaping the 20th century. One hundred years ago, the American eugenics movement played a major role in shaping the philosophy of both the field of education and politics. This started as a relatively small but well-funded movement and went on to manifest itself in unspeakable horrors in the Nazi Death camps. It is widely known that Hitler collaborated with some of the leaders of the American eugenicist movement. By 1934, the *Richmond Times-Dispatch* quoted a prominent American eugenicist as saying, "The Germans are beating us at our own game" (Delegates urge wider practice of sterilization, 1934). In fact, Hitler directly stated that "the Germanic inhabitant of the American continent, who has remained racially pure and unmixed, rose to be master of the continent; he will remain the master as long as he does not fall a victim to defilement of the blood" (1925, Vol.1, Ch.11).

Henry Goddard was one of the prominent voices in the American eugenics movement. In 1936, he sent the results of some of his eugenics experiments to Otto Verschuer and Joseph Mengele, two of Nazi Germany's behavioral scientists who were directly involved with the heinous campaign of "racial hygiene" (Black, 2003, p. 342). Previous to this, Goddard had already been instrumental in the development of intelligence testing and was using it in a government-sponsored program of screening out "mental defectives" at Ellis Island. This was deemed necessary because in the United States, during the early 1900s, a large influx of a wide variety of ethnic groups created issues of "population control," paving the way for an undue emphasis on the biological nature of intelligence. In 1920, Goddard published *Human Efficiency and Levels of Intelligence*. His ideas acted as a catalyst for the creation of IQ tests that were first used to screen out "mental defectives" for deportation or forced sterilization. Goddard viewed intelligence as a complete product of nature. He states his position on the first page of the book: "The mental level for each individual is determined by the kind chromosomes that come together with the union of the germ cells: that it is but little affected by any later influences except serious accidents as may destroy part of the mechanism" (p. 1).

Consequently, Zenderland (1998) reported that "the number of immigrants who were deported increased exponentially as a result of these screening measures" (p. 268). The views espoused by Goddard and other like-minded eugenicists continued to hold sway, as evidenced by the rise of fascism in Europe and the laissez-faire attitudes expressed in social Darwinism. It was only after a worldwide public outcry and the Nuremberg trials (1945–1949) that the eugenics movement began to lose momentum. However, the more covert aspects of this legacy are still very much alive in the present emphasis on individual performance as measured through standardized intelligence testing.

During World War II, intelligence testing became widespread after being administered to over 1.7 million U.S. Army recruits (Fancher, 1985). The results of this study bolstered the use of the IQ test for job screening and educational placement. The extensive use of intelligence tests led to the creation of a "one curriculum for leadership and another for [followership]" (Kliebard, 1986, p. 111). Military officers, executives, and students were all chosen and placed in their "genetically determined destinies," and many others were turned away because of a low "intelligence quotient."

By 1945 there were so many students in America who had been excluded from the college preparatory track of education that a completely new curriculum was created, called "life adjustment" education. This curriculum of "followership" and the ensuing tracking policies were constant reminders to those of us who were so placed that this is where we "belonged." This perception is part of what keeps the "banking model" of education going. In his discussion of the tactics of the oppressor as a cultural invader, Freire says that the "invaded become convinced of their own intrinsic inferiority" (1970, p. 153). Testing has often served to convince individuals that they belong where they are in the grand scheme of things.

I vividly recall my own experience in this situation when I was in the tenth grade. I was placed in a social studies class for slow readers because of test scores and my academic record. Recently, I obtained all my K–12 transcripts. I discovered that I was tracked to "Group two" in first grade reading. Needless to say, I was not expected to attend college. I also researched my test scores for that period. According to the way test results were interpreted at that time, I certainly should not be teaching at the university level. My scores place me in a category along with: "machine operators; shopkeepers; butchers; welders; sheet metal workers" (Wilson & Grylls, 1977).

By the tenth grade, I was in the "industrial arts" track social studies class where we were given the answers to questions for tests a day ahead of time. I remember the shame I experienced at times at having to attend these classes. I have already mentioned the caring teacher who intervened on my behalf because he saw my potential as a person and knew some of my family history. There was no magic that turned me into an instant academic wonder, but I do think about that experience quite often when working with my students. More often than not, the boost they need comes from sensitive teachers who see beyond numbers and essentialist labels. Conversely, the only way that atrocities like the horrors of the Holocaust could have taken place was to label the victims as "subhuman" and completely objectify and abstract their existence. This is the ultimate expression of "seeing things small."

However, dehumanization even in a small way is something that all of us need to guard against. One very poignant quote in this connection comes from what Freire said in response to a 10-year-old boy's questions and comments at dinner attended by some prominent leaders in education, including Maxine Greene. "Be quiet [spoken to the adults]. Every time you ignore a person's question, you dehumanize them" (Quoted in Wink, 2000, p. 80).

Walls of Fragmentation Between Subjects

The Tylerian paradigm took definitive form in 1949 with the publication of *Basic Principles of Curriculum and Instruction*. The influence of Tyler's work practically dominated the curriculum field for the rest of the 20th century. As the '40s closed, the influence and "the growth of experientialist curriculum thought was temporarily halted," and basic skills were stressed with fervor (Schubert, Lopez-Schubert, Thomas, & Carroll, 2002, p. 97). These skills were taught as isolated disciplines with little or no connection between subjects. Each one had to be mastered in a linear lockstep fashion. It is very striking indeed to see how little of this has changed in fifty plus years! In some cases, there is even more fragmentation now than there was in 1949. At least many of those in school had other duties outside the classroom that gave them an opportunity to learn many things from experience through interaction with nature or creating things in the home.

Now with such high stakes associated with standardized tests scores, some schools have divided their school days between two subjects: math and reading. According to a recent survey conducted by the Center on Education Policy, "since the passage of the federal law, 71 percent of the nation's 15,000 school districts had reduced the hours of instructional time spent on history, music and other subjects to open up more time for reading and math" (Dillon, 2006).

When these subjects are decontextualized and fragmented, students lose motivation and interest in what could otherwise open up worlds of personal meaning to them. "Only two subjects? What a sadness," said Thomas Sobol, an education professor at Columbia Teachers College and a former

New York State education commissioner. "That's like a violin student who's only permitted to play scales, nothing else, day after day, scales, scales, scales. They'd lose their zest for music" (Dillon, 2006).

In a similar way, imagine a basketball player who is told that he must improve his fundamentals, so instead of being allowed to play in a real game, the only thing that he is allowed to do is practice layup shots and run up and down the court. Both these examples are apt at describing the effects of fragmentation because they point to the absurdity of isolating subject matter apart from the big picture of the entire world of music in the first instance and the spontaneous adventure of interactive participation in a game of basketball in the second instance. Yet for many, that is exactly what school has been like for over a hundred years!

David Orr (1994) offers valuable insight into the nature of real intelligence as being vastly different from simply being "clever." Cleverness is what enables the regurgitation of facts and decontextualized bits of information. I know many people who have never been considered "successful" in school but are really brilliant just the same, because they have "know how" (Orr, 1994, p. 49) through experiential knowledge that is in harmony with its surroundings. This is vastly different than having information!

The business model of education has narrowed and undermined intelligence to mean the "answers to other people's questions, when it is only a means to achieve preordained goals" (Orr, 1994, p. 29). Standardized testing is producing standardized, known quantities in students and teachers. This results in the discounting of real intelligence by dulling or outright destroying the desire to discover, on one's own terms, the areas of inquiry that are truly a personal delight.

In contrast to standardized information, Pinar (2004) wonderfully describes how "knowledge and intelligence as free exploration become wings by which we take flight, visit other worlds, returning to this one to call others, especially our children, to futures more life-affirmative than the world we inhabit now" (p. 31).

Sputnik and Increased Meritocracy

With the threat of nuclear war and the "race for space" came the so-called Sputnik curriculum era, with its teacher-proof curriculum in math and science and the corresponding increase in national standardized test scores. A reaction to the "watered down oversimplification of the topics" (Schubert et al., 2002, p. 120) that came in with the life-adjustment curriculum of the 1940s gave rise to a renewed emphasis on the traditionalist disciplines.

In addition, the behaviorist paradigm took on new strength with the publication of B. F. Skinner's *Science and Human Behavior* in 1953. His views bolstered the increased emphasis on tracking and the standardizing of education in general. Conant wrote *The American High School Today* in 1959. With the publication of this book, Conant sought to reinforce a multilayered high school program that would "facilitate general education, college preparation, and the gamut of vocational education simultaneously, with special attention to cultivating the most able" (Schubert et al., 2002, p. 128).

In spite of claims of inclusion and "progress" for all, tracking has always been based on statistical outcomes, and, though the labels for it are changed every few years, standardized tests are used as a means of reinforcing the stratification of our culture. As Sacks (1999) suggests in his book, *Standardized Minds*, this hegemonic control is maintained by redefining what it means to have "merit."

> Most people would agree that, in a democracy, merit is a good basis for deciding who gets ahead. The rub is how you define merit. We have settled on a system that defines merit in large part as the "potential" to achieve according to test results. It turns out that the lion's share of the potential in our society goes to those with well-to-do, highly educated parents. The aristocracy also used to perpetuate itself on the basis of birth and parentage. But the nation's elites now perpetuate their class privilege with rules of their own making that have persisted for several decades, rules legitimated and protected by a pseudoscientific objectivity. (p. 15)

The catch-22 of all this is that that many of these same schools are spending an inordinate amount of time on standardized test preparation in order to qualify for the funding that they need to provide the milieu that inspires students toward imaginative engagement and aesthetic educational activities. These areas of the curriculum are the first to go. Nevertheless, "merit" is still measured by test scores.

The implementation of these various programs served to reproduce and reinforce the class structure in the entire culture. You do not have to look very far to see the evidence of this concept. Indeed, this system tends to reinforce the kind of essentialist views that eventually contributed to the level of school violence that has brought such a terrible disfigurement to our nation.

A Brief Glimpse Beyond the Wall

The 1960s brought about many changes in every part of our culture. Models of intelligence had already been broadened by the work of Piaget and other developmental psychologists (Schubert et al., 2002). By 1960, Behaviorism took a hard hit through the work of Chomsky (1959) and others who argued for an innate faculty for learning language. Chomsky holds the notion that humans are hardwired for language acquisition. This hypothesis based on his explanation for the human ability to string new sentences together that had never been uttered before. This is in contrast to learning language as habit formation by the stimulus-response method.

Even so, this theory hardly stopped the great move toward "business-like specification of objectives" (Schubert et al., 2002, p. 151) that picked up steam through this decade. Schubert et al. further report on the same page that *Preparing Instructional Objectives* (Mager, 1962) was written to:

> move those who wrote objectives away from the use of vague terms with multiple interpretations. The immense popularity of the above book, however, produced staunch proponents of this new approach, who rejected goal statements that had even a tinge of vagueness, lacked time specifications, lacked definitive criteria for evaluation, or failed to specify results in observable (and hopefully reasonable) behaviors.

In spite of this, the call from "above the walls" began to be heard by a growing number, as many traditional views throughout our culture were being questioned. The 1960s closed with the youth revolution in full force. For a vast number of baby boomers, there could be no return to the status quo. The culture was ripe for wholesale changes in philosophy and education. Pinar, Reynolds, Slattery, and Taubman (1995) observed, "By the early 1970s, the field was 'up for grabs'. Schwab's declaration that the field was 'moribund' struck a deep chord" (p. 187). They was not alone in this observation. By the middle of the decade, there were many leading voices in education echoing this response.

Walls of "Excellence"

The publication of *A Nation at Risk* (U.S. National Commission on Excellence, 1984) was supposed to counteract the decline in public schools that was brought on by "experientialist educators of the late 1960s and 1970s who were alleged to have sacrificed academic rigor for fuzzy humanistic social development" (Schubert et al., 2002, p. 258). A movement to provide "excellence" in education paralleled the realm of business practices that were "in search of excellence" (Peters & Waterman, 1982). This book was written to highlight the management methods of America's best-run companies.

There was a real concern at that time that other nations would surpass the United States in economic and academic achievement. All of this led to a renewed emphasis in "basic skills," especially in math and science. The factory model had found a new incarnation in the "excellence in education" motif.

The paradigm wars continued through this decade as agents of the Clinton administration pushed for a national standardized curriculum and increased accountability measured by standardized tests. This move followed on the heels of the conditions that ensued during the previous decade with the publication of A *Nation at Risk* (U.S. National Commission on Excellence, 1984) and coalesced around the *Goals 2000: Educate America Act* (U.S. Department of Education, 1994).

The term "benchmarks" for each grade level became the new buzzword. This word was adapted from the field of business, to insure the standardized implementation of known quantities throughout a specific industry. As the business model infiltrates the field of education, even Kindergarten students become the objects of benchmarking.

As the last century came to a close, Schubert et al. (2002) reported that the concept of benchmarking was enacted at the state level almost across the board by way of "the promotion of state achievement testing of students to ensure that they had attained the content standards based on elaborate state goals set forth in nearly every state" (p. 353). The textbooks publishers saw this as a goose that laid golden eggs and responded with another wave of "teacher-proof" curriculum (Apple & Christian-Smith, 1991, quoted in Schubert et al., 2002). I will elaborate further on the big business of testing under the section on the No Child Left Behind Act of 2003.

The New Eugenics

The publication of *The Bell Curve* (Herrnstein & Murray, 1994) launched a debate on the nature of biological intelligence that refueled a controversy that goes back to Goddard and the social Darwinists. The authors see little need to educate those with lower IQs for jobs that require the type of intelligence that is favored by intelligence tests, as seen in the following quote from the book:

These possibilities all bear on a crucial issue: How much good would it do to encourage education for the people earning low wages? If somehow [government] can cajole or entice youths to stay in school for a few extra years, will their economic disadvantage in the new labor market go away? We doubt it. Their disadvantage might be diminished, but only modestly. There is reason to think that the job market has been rewarding not just education but intelligence. (p. 96)

No wonder nihilism and even suicide are on the rise among African American teens (West, 1994). The narrowing of the "way out" and the shrinking presence of positive role models are factors that have contributed to a sharp increase in suicidal deaths in this group. Here is an excerpt from a transcript of "The NewsHour with Jim Lehrer":

While suicide was once relatively rare among black teenagers, a study just released by the Center for Disease Control shows over the last two decades it has increased dramatically. The study found that while the suicide rate for white youth is still higher than for African American youth, the rate of suicide for African Americans is rising much faster. From 1980 to 1994, the suicide rate for whites age 15 to 19 went up 22 percent, while the rate for 15 to 19 year old blacks increased by 146 percent. (Winslow & McCleery, 1998)

Unless one has the cultural capital that is needed to play the academic game, his or her options become slimmer and slimmer. Even those who "make it" are aware that this is often at the expense of personal creativity and even identity. The kind of intelligence that is measured on any standardized test is narrowly defined to an academic meta-language that opens or closes the doors for people of any race. The 2003 nationwide high school graduation rates of African-American students further reveal the crisis in this age group: "While 59 percent of African-American females graduated, only 48 percent of African-American males earned a diploma" (Greene & Winters, 2005). This is tragic indeed! One reason for this is because, for the most part, standardized schooling fails to engage our youth because the content is boring and "one size fits few" (Ohanian, 1999).

The Mega-Business of Building Walls

The current testing climate has provided a gold mine to those in the textbook publishing business. The market for "painting by numbers" curriculum design appears to be a steady growth industry. Consider the excerpt from the following article in *Corpwatch*. Sales of printed materials related to standardized tests nearly tripled from 1992 to last year, jumping from $211 million to $592 million, according to the American Association of

Publishers. Three corporate giants dominate both testing and textbooks: CTB-McGraw Hill, Harcourt (owned by London-based Reed Elsevier), and Houghton Mifflin, which together control about 80% of the market. The total market in textbooks and related educational materials is over $7 billion (Clarke, 2004). This explosive growth ensued as a result of increased pressure to "upgrade" educational standards through the Goals 2000: Educate America act of 1994 legacy followed by the current No Child Left Behind bandwagon. These trends were also intensified at the state and local levels through the introduction of specified benchmark programs such as Georgia's Quality Core Curriculum (Georgia Department of Education, 2008) standards and high school graduation tests. These changes have often resulted in the formation of a culture of test preparation in schools that unseats the kind of environment that is conducive to real learning. For example, there are recent reports of from teachers in a large school district in the south that teachers are written up if they go three minutes past the scripted lesson plan. In the same school district, playground equipment that was given to the school is still in the delivery boxes because test preparation leaves no time for recess.

One specific example of an individual who has earned millions from all sides of the testing industry as both a lobbyist and a consultant is a Dallas lawyer and colleague of G.W. Bush named Sandy Kress. He is one of the main authors of the No Child Left Behind Act of 2003 and is one of the chief proponents of one of the most recent buzzwords in education: accountability. According to Kress, "the best hope for poor and minority students, lies in the public humiliation of their [low performing] schools" (Pyle, 2005, p. 1).

Of course, the next step involves "supplying the demand public school reform has created for tests and the tools it takes to pass them" (Pyle, 2005, p. 2). This is where Kress has found multiple sources of income that all connect with each other in his bank account. Kress has served as a lobbyist for McGraw-Hill, and five months after the passage of NCLB, he became a lobbyist for NCS Pearson, "the third largest testing company in the country" (Pyle, 2005, p. 5). The company also offers professional training for teachers to use their testing software. Other clients of the Kress lobbying cash machine are Educational Testing Service, which is now entering the state-level testing market. He also is a lobbyist for Kaplan Incorporated, which is now is one of the major producers of "skill-drilling software, and professional development courses in which, for roughly $1000 an hour, Kaplan specialists give teachers tips on how to coach their students to pass the test" (Pyle, 2005, p. 6). So, like so many other aspects of business, the field of education has fallen prey to the trend of creating needs that did not exist and then selling the means to meet the artificially created needs with materials that are labeled "authentic" or "research-based." Meanwhile, in spite of the frenzy of testing and retesting, teaching to the tests, and retesting again, long-term trends show no significant increase in learning. Reynolds (2003) offers an astute observation to explain why the current administration persists in its push for higher statistical results.

> Why the infatuation with testing? For its most conservative enthusiasts, testing makes sense as a lone solution to school failure because, they insist, adequate resources are already in place, and only the threat of exposure and censure is necessary for schools to succeed. Moreover, among those who style themselves as "compassionate conservatives," education has become sentimental and, all things considered, a cheap way to talk about equalizing opportunity without committing to substantial income redistribution. Liberal faddishness, not chronic under funding of poorer schools or child poverty itself, is blamed for underachievement: "Child-centered" education, "progressive" education or "Whole language"—each has been singled out as a social menace that can be vanquished only by applying a more rational, results-oriented and business-minded approach to education. (p. 70)

Students as Human Capital

The curriculum of "followership" (Kliebard, 1986, p. 111) serves the interests of the globalization of business quite well. I saw this play out recently on a trip to a certain retail super center. I entered the store holding a medium sized poster that announced a blood bank visit to the school where I work and went straight to the service desk. After introducing myself and pointing to the poster, I asked for permission to display it. A series of four people were consulted, all with various supervisory capacities. Finally, one of them informed me that their superior was in a meeting and that I would have to wait to get his permission. I asked if I could leave the poster with her because I had to get back to work myself, and if the supervisor said no to my request, then I gave them permission to throw the poster away.

What struck me the most about that experience is that people are being trained not to think or question. That concept took me right back to Freire's (1970) statement about the effects of banking education: "The capability of banking education, to minimize or annul the students' creative power and to stimulate their credulity, serves the interests of the oppressors" (p. 73). The idea of students as compliant human capital is frightening indeed! But this is part of the hidden curriculum of the accountability movement in education.

As the 20th century came to a close, the field of economics began to look for ways to standardize the value of human productivity. The criteria that are now in place look remarkably similar to the benchmark system of student assessment.

In a book called *The ROI of Human Capital: Measuring the Economic Value of Employee Performance*, (2000) Fitz-Enz quotes Rummler and Brache as saying that "measurement is *the* pivotal performance management and improvement tool and as such deserves special treatment" (p. 4). Performance and management are measured by effective accomplishment of tasks and execution of orders, attitudes of compliance, and other "work ethics issues." The author further explains that employee performance should be compared to a standard or a benchmark. He sums up these statements by saying that "if we don't know how to measure our primary value-producing asset, we can't manage it" (Fitz-Enz, 2000, p. 4). Please notice that people are referred to as "it." Incidentally, "ROI" is an acronym for "return on investment," which is exactly what the federal government wants to see in terms of standardized test scores. But what is really measured on these tests is individual test taking ability!

However, it is not my purpose to completely discard the use of numerical measurement. When we look at who is actually inventing or creating new products, we have a solid indicator of the effects of a standardized culture. How about this for a statistic? According to the United States Patent and Trademark Office (2006), in 2004, 48% of the United States patents granted were of foreign origin. That share has been increasing for years. In 1964, it was 18%, and in 1974, that figure was 33%.

I once heard of a Saint Bernard puppy that grew up behind a fence. He grew to be about twice as high as the fence, but because he had lived his whole life in confinement, he never realized that he could just step right into freedom. Need I say more?

3

Metaphor

The Language of the Imagination

*Metaphor is the great human revolution; at least on a par with the invention
of the wheel. . . . Metaphor is a weapon in the hand-to-hand struggle with reality.*
—Yehuda Amichai (Quoted in Gussow, 2000).

The Unfinished Conversation Continues

Paulo: Maxine, you have thought and written extensively on the domain of metaphor. What connections exist between imagination
and making metaphors?

Maxine: "By means of making metaphors, imagination can reorient
consciousness through its disclosure of patterns, relationships,
shadows, and lights, and slivers of sound that are wholly unexpected, 'new' in fashion" (Greene, 2001, p. 154).

Paulo: Yes, I can see that! The familiar becomes my new metaphoric
extension. One of the primary means I have used in teaching
literacy in Brazil is built on using metaphoric concepts from the
students' own world of language. I use carefully selected pictures

A Curriculum of Imagination in an Era of Standardization, pages 29–41
Copyright © 2013 by Information Age Publishing
All rights of reproduction in any form reserved.

of generative metaphoric concepts that have indeed enabled the reorienting of consciousness in creative and critical ways.

Maxine: How interesting! I understand that you take a video camera into the villages before you begin teaching, in order to capture pictures of some of these metaphoric concepts. What are some examples you have used?

Paulo: I use a picture of a man and a woman working near a well as metaphors that express "the distinction of two worlds: that of nature and that of culture" (Freire, 2007, p. 42). This is done by asking questions like, "Who made the well? Why did he do it? How did he do it? When?" (p. 63). Out of this framework, we talk about the man's relation to the world and how, through his work, he transforms the world. We also discuss relations among men, not as objects but subjects. It is amazing to witness how much of the world the students already "read" in metaphoric representation. Reading and writing flow naturally out of these metaphoric concepts.

Maxine: I do something very similar with metaphor in the domain of literature and art. By these means, students are able to overcome their sense of powerlessness when confronting a "predefined world, marked off and explained by others (usually others whom they do not know, and who do not have their interests at heart)" (Greene, 2001, p. 137).

Paulo: That is a very powerful motivator for literacy. Students learn to read and write by being enabled to tell their own stories, come to their own conclusions, and name their worlds!

Maxine: It takes metaphor to

> transform memory into a principle of continuity in experience. I think that, like me . . . you are able to reach back and find out (especially when you shape your narratives, tell your stories) how understandings are made possible by art experiences that help you identify the themes, to articulate the hidden moments of your lives. (Greene, 2001, p. 103)

Paulo: Yes! The key to releasing students from the walls of the "banking model of education" (Freire, 1970) is to enable them to recognize and then break with *prescription* and with the notion of "predefinition" that you expressed so well. That is what imagination expressing itself through metaphor does best.

Orwell's Newspeak and Standardization

The reduction of knowledge to singular standardized outcomes and one-dimensional meanings on multiple-choice tests is a frightful reminder of the Orwellian concept of Newspeak from *Nineteen Eighty-Four*. In Newspeak, "all ambiguities and shades of meaning" (Orwell, 1949, p. 304) are purged from languages so that one word conveys one rigidly defined thought. This made the use of words impossible for anything except daily routines. Freedom for example, could only mean one thing. Orwell gives an example of this one-dimensional aspect of freedom in Newspeak by saying, "The dog is free of lice" (p. 304). In Big Brother's kingdom, this word carried no other connotations. The realm of metaphor therefore was obsolete and forbidden.

Even though *Nineteen Eighty Four* is a novel, it does reflect periods in human history that did not look kindly on the use of metaphor. In fact, it is only recently that metaphor has earned the respect of scientists, mathematicians, and psychologists, as well as linguists and poets. Sadly, the field of education is one of the last to see the value of metaphor, yet education is one of the areas where it is needed the most.

What is Metaphor?

The word metaphor comes from the combination of the Greek words *meta*, which means "over," and *pherein*, "to carry" (Hawkes, 1972, p. 1). This "carrying over" describes the blending of the features of one concept to another in a unique combination that results in a new shade of meaning. *By this action, the creator of metaphor transcends walls of limited expression into personal sense making and identity.* Richards (1936) astutely describes the structure of metaphor as "two thoughts of different things active together and supported by a single word, or phrase, whose meaning is a resultant of their interaction" (p. 93).

Lakoff and Johnson (1980/2003) express this interaction as more than just the combination of the names of objects at the sentence level. Their emphasis is more on the conjoined meaning of concepts within the context of lived experience when they write that "the essence of metaphor is understanding and experiencing one kind of thing in terms of another" (p. 5).

The traditional view of metaphor is that it is a form of figurative language that is used to dress up the literal usage of words and phrases. Many still view metaphor as fanciful or not really essential to basic communication. In the last half of the 20th century, this notion has been reexamined in the fields of psychology, neuroscience, philosophy, and linguistics. From these disciplines, a growing consensus suggests that metaphor is fundamental to the process of thinking and communicating. Lakoff and Johnson (1980/2003) express the tenor of these views when they say that "our conceptual system is largely metaphorical" (p. 3). This view includes both conscious and subconscious thought expressed outwardly in words that tie concepts together into one expression.

For example, if I say "a tidal wave of weariness hit me yesterday afternoon," the person I am addressing gets a fuller picture than if I simply said, "I was very tired yesterday afternoon." By combining the image of a tidal wave with the condition of tiredness, a fuller and more personalized description emerges. Through metaphor, both conscious and subconscious thought are combined with past and present experience in defining moments that create personal meaning and signature. Here is a closer look at the example from my baseball experience that I briefly mentioned in the prologue.

Metaphor Defined by Personal Experience

Crack! The baseball connected with the sweet spot on the bat, and the ball sailed over the left field fence and nearly made it to the roof of the waterworks building that was located about 25 feet beyond the baseball field. I was only 11 years old, small for my age, and more surprised by the trajectory path of the ball than anyone on the field. I had hit a home run! The bigger guys on both teams could hardly believe it. I also took note, with great satisfaction, that one of the cutest girls in the whole town witnessed my triumph as well. For a brief period after that, my self-confidence soared.

At the time, I had no idea what a defining moment that homerun swing would become for me through the course of my life. I have literally dreamt hundreds of times about hitting a homerun in a major league baseball stadium. This dream has occurred more frequently during my doctoral studies than anytime I can remember. Sometimes I wake up in the middle of this recurring dream and find myself saying, "I'm gonna knock the ball into the middle of next week!" In the last year or so, my dream has become more interactive. I find that I am able to adjust my swing to the velocity and location of the ball and still manage to swat it over the left field fence without fail. Hitting a homerun has become a personal metaphor for overcoming obstacles, but more than this, it is a part of my inner language of motivation. Now, I hope I continue to have this dream for the rest of my life. In fact, if I stopped dreaming it, I would be concerned.

Every person's inner landscape is unique. Some people are influenced more by their waking acts of cogitation than by what they dream. There is an infinitively wide range of sources of inner language emerging from the combined factors of nature and experience. Metaphor brings all these connections together in imagination. Indeed, metaphor is the very language of the imagination, or I should say, it expresses the multiple languages of the imagination that include visual, numerical, musical, somatic, and rhythmic expression. I will explore this in greater detail in the next chapter. Before that, I need to connect to the historical evolution of metaphor and then move forward into new places of discovery.

Two Trees of Developing Metaphor

The history of the use of metaphor parallels the history of the imagination in many respects. This is because the use of metaphor figures so prominently into the exercise of the imagination. Indeed, one of the greatest "tools" used in imaginative construction of meaning is metaphor. When one considers the historical meanings of both, it becomes clear that when the work of the imagination is valued, so also is the use of metaphor.

Johnson (1981) outlines four paradigms in the development of metaphor that are worth considering. Instead of labeling these linear periods, they are better thought of as cultural paradigms because they all exist together at present. Some are obviously more evolved than others, so it is necessary to delineate them. Johnson begins his history with Greek thought, followed by the classical and medieval paradigms. Modernism is an extension of these.

I now want to offer a metaphor on the development of metaphor. I see all these paradigms as two different trees. One I call the Cartesian tree, which is rooted in Greek thought. The trunk consists of classical, medieval, and modern thought. From there, it stems into positivism, behaviorism, some aspects of cognitive psychology, and standardization. The fruit is measured and tasted for "norm referencing." The colors are mediocre, and the taste is flat.

The other one I call the Vico tree. The roots of this tree go back to the very beginning of the human family in what has been called "preliterate culture." The trunk has the Romantic poets to thank for its life. The branches grow in an existential environment that is neither modern nor postmodern, pushing upward and outward into creative and critical symmetry. Every limb has its own unique story and is expressed in an infinite variety of cultural expression by every medium that is presently known to the human family, as well as an infinite expression of the yet unnamed and uncreated growth. The fruit is all wonderfully diverse in every way, engulfing all experience of taste and fragrance. The whole spectrum of human experience grows in astonishing and, at times, even wild symmetry, just waiting for partakers to experience and personalize.

Metaphor in Preliterate Cultures

Ancient cultures used metaphor in word pictures and gestures as well as in symbolic dances and facial expressions. There is a great deal of evidence from the fields of linguistics and cognitive psychology that suggests the co-evolution of language and metaphor (Modell, 2003). This hypothesis seems plausible when there is still so much nonverbal metaphoric communication in every culture at present.

One example that comes to mind immediately is the metaphor for murder that is expressed by dragging the index finger across the neck. This can mean that a child is in big trouble with his parents, or that an employee is about to be fired, or in some cases literal death.

Native Americans used metaphoric gesture in their dance rituals. These practices date back to preliterate periods, although some contemporary tribes have preserved some aspects of this phenomenon. According to Warburg (1995), as late as the 19th century, the Pueblo Indians used live rattlesnakes as a metaphor for lightning in their rain dances because the snakes move in a zigzag pattern that resembles the shape of lightning flashes.

It is likely that sign language was used before written and spoken language, and it is now well established that sign language is rich with the use of newly created metaphor. One illustration of this is the sign for "think-hearing." This word transfers the sign for "hearing" (a finger rotating near the mouth) to the region of the head in order to describe someone who thinks and acts like a non-deaf person (Davidson, 2002, p. 76).

The value of considering past and present uses of preliterate metaphor is that they suggest to us that the connections between the body and mind are much stronger than what has been accepted up until now. Many aspects of the use of metaphor emerge through connecting the physical world with the inner world of conscious and unconscious thought.

Lakoff and Johnson (1999) propose that our conceptual system is shaped by both our sensorimotor and cognitive experiences. Some of the examples include "affection is warmth." This comes from feeling warm by being held affectionately. Another one is "difficulties are burdens." This, of course, is the result of the experience of lifting heavy objects. And "knowing is seeing" comes from our experience of obtaining information through the eyes. These examples characterize the connections between body and mind and at the same time imply to us that primary metaphorical experience is the gateway to more advanced connections required in spoken and written communication.

Metaphor in the Greek and Medieval Cultures

Until Socrates, there was a natural view of metaphor in the poetry and mythology of the Ancient world. Plato's view of the inferiority of imitation in poetry led him to view metaphor as an obstruction to truth. However, there is an irony here, as Johnson (1981) points out: Plato's "critique of imitative poetry has often been read as applying to metaphor generally, despite his supreme use of metaphor to convey most of his philosophical convictions" (p. 5).

Aristotle gave more importance to metaphor but still viewed it as fanciful or ornamental (Hestor, 1967). Through Aristotle's view, the literal versus figurative dichotomy takes on a new dimension and exerts an influence on Western philosophy even up to the present time. And although Aristotle values the rhetorical aspect of figurative language, he limits the use of metaphor by basing its use on the similarity of two elements. In *The Rhetoric*, he says that metaphors "like epithets, must be fitting, which means they must fairly correspond to the thing signified: failing this, their inappropriateness will be conspicuous" (n.d., 1405a). This view tends to weaken the use of metaphor by treating it as "mere comparison with no distinctive cognitive function" (Johnson, 1981, p. 9).

One of the reasons that metaphor contributes so much to personal sense making is that it can bring elements together that have no categorical relationship except in the experience of the creator of the metaphor. For example, what relationship does fog have to cats? In Carl Sandburg's mind, there is a very strong one.

> *Fog*
> The fog comes
> on little cat feet.
> It sits looking
> over harbor and city
> on silent haunches
> and then moves on
> (1970, p. 33)

Not only does metaphor enable the connection of completely disparate concepts, it also carries the ability to create new concepts and worlds of meaning. This notion reminds me of James Dickey's last lecture on poetry at the University of South Carolina, just a short time before his death, which his son quotes verbatim in his memoirs. Here the emphasis is on the power of metaphor to express thoughts through personal interpretation:

> We are secondary creators. We take God's universe and make it over in some way. And it is different from His. It is similar in some ways, but it is different in some ways. And the difference lies in the slant, in the slant that we individually put on it. That is the difference. That is where our value lies. Not only for ourselves, but for the other people who read us. There is some increment there that we make possible that would not otherwise be there. (Dickey, 1998, p. 269)

The medieval paradigm stands in stark contrast to this. Aristotle's views helped shape medieval thought, largely through the influence his philosophy held over the Church of Rome. From the position of having a "divine right" to decide what was true, the church "mounted a new attack on the embellishment of language in general" (Johnson, 1981, p. 9). During that period, it was feared that speakers might get too free and indulge in pagan excess with their tongues. The influence of the monastic life widened the dichotomy of mind and body. Metaphors were accepted in scripture but were regarded as a means of obscuring the truth in any other use. Johnson (1981) succinctly sums up the view of metaphor in the ancient and medieval periods when describing the prevailing view that "metaphor is a deviant use of a word to point up similarities" (p. 11).

Metaphor in Modern Philosophy

The Enlightenment period did little to advance the use of metaphor. In fact, it was viewed with suspicion rather than appreciation by the men who began the rationalist/empiricist movement. Hobbes thought that "metaphors, and senseless and ambiguous words, are like *ignes fatui*; and reasoning upon them is wandering amongst innumerable absurdities; and their end, contention and sedition, or contempt" (1834/2004, p. 17). These views are echoed in Locke and Descartes as well. These men were all in search of a purely objective epistemology that left almost nothing to the realm of the imagination or the senses. Descartes actually sought to "mathematize the human mind" (Modell, 2003, p. 6). Sadly, this legacy continues on in the present movement of standardization and the computational view of the mind, which is still found in many circles of cognitive psychology.

Romantic Use of Metaphor

Into this sensory vacuum came the Romantic movement. It is no surprise that along with a renewed interest in the poetic imagination through Kant, Coleridge, and Wordsworth, the use of metaphor was elevated to new heights. One man who is rarely mentioned, whose views are strikingly similar to forward thinkers at the end of the 20th century, is Giambattista Vico. In fact, his work helped to spark the Romantic movement by influencing the poets and writers of the late Eighteenth century. In his work called *New Science* (1744), he states that "it is noteworthy that in all language, the greater part of the expressions relating to inanimate things is formed by metaphors from the human body and its parts and from the human senses and passions" (p. 405). In Vico's view, this formation of the mind through language began through metaphorical signs and gestures. Metaphor became the primary way of knowing and understanding experience in the world.

Modell (2003) acknowledges the importance Vico placed on this view by saying that "metaphor was understood not as a figure of speech, a trope, but as a vital means of understanding the world" (p. 15). Vico's views sound remarkably like Dewey (1934), Greene (1995), and others who welcome a pluralistic epistemology through the portals of the body/mind. The modern period's view of metaphor is an ongoing phenomenon. The two trees represented by Vico and Descartes have branched out in a variety of directions in the present day.

Metaphor Today

In the 20th century, branches from the Cartesian tree spread their boughs in positivism and behaviorism and in some aspects of cognitive psychology that view the computer as a model for the operation of the human mind. Positivism has no use for metaphor because it is predicated on the belief that all "scientific knowledge can be reduced to a system of literal and verifiable sentences" (Johnson, 1981, p. 17). In behaviorism, only quantifiable outcomes are relevant. While cognitive psychology acknowledges some aspects of brain lateralization, creativity, and problem solving, it rejects an emphasis on the subconscious. Even Chomsky, with his formal rules of syntax in his theory of universal grammar, represents another bough of the Cartesian tree stemming out of the cognitive psychology branch.

In the climate of positivism, the Vico tree appeared to be stunted in growth or even barren in last part of the 19th century and early 20th century. In 1936, however, I. A. Richards published his *Philosophy of Rhetoric*, a work that grew directly out of Vico's thinking. Richards broadsided the literal truth paradigm when he expressed his view that metaphor is at the basis of all thought. "Thought is metaphoric, and proceeds by comparison, and the metaphors of language derive therefrom" (Richards, 1936, p. 94). In other words, he believed that at the base of all thinking, there is a metaphoric relationship. Richards takes this one step further when he suggests that metaphors are "cognitively irreducible" (Johnson, 1981, p. 19) or cannot be reduced to statements of literal meaning. A metaphoric expression therefore becomes a newly created vehicle of meaning that loses potency when seeking to make a literal statement out of its component parts.

As an example of this, I am reminded of a lecture I heard once by Akeroyd (1986). In his presentation, he removed all of the metaphorical references in Frost's "The Road Not Taken." It is hard to imagine this without metaphor, but it was something like, "I came to a fork in the road, and I took the one that had less traffic, and things worked out all right." Literalism destroys the medium and the message and blocks the multiple dimensions of rich interpretation, robbing the imagination of its greatest power as a generative interpreter of experience. Black (1954/1955) goes so far as to say that in some cases, metaphors create new meaning rather than just offering a means of expressing old ideas in a new way.

Needless to say, these ideas were not readily welcomed by the prevailing cultures that were (and still are) dominated by the age of science. Nevertheless, in the latter half of the 20th century, the metaphor tree began to take shape and branch out into philosophy, neuroscience, psychology, and education. The work of Freud and Jung found their antecedents in the concept of metaphor. The field of neuroscience brought about a domain of study that offered neural connections as a possible explanation to the bringing together of disparate elements in metaphor. The field of philosophy found new territory by viewing the body and mind holistically, thus making dualism obsolete, or at least not as relevant to present views of epistemology. This notion was further strengthened by feminist scholars who eschewed the objectification of the body and the dualism that exists in the Cartesian analysis of the mind as distinct from the body. Eventually, the field of education also found a measure of receptivity to the synthesis of body and mind in personal discovery of the self and ultimately in the use of metaphor for narrative inquiry.

Educational uses of metaphor provide a way to bring this inquiry up to the present, so I will focus on this domain from this point onward. In particular, I center on the field of curriculum studies because what actually takes place in schools starts with the way we think, and circumscribed horizons of thought lead to imprisoning practices. It is also interesting to note that the word "curriculum" is itself a metaphor, a "course to be run" (Lawton, 1984,

p. 79). Indeed, from the early 1970s to the present, the field of curriculum study has become a significant bough of metaphoric expression with a wide variety of extending branches.

Metaphors and Education

By the mid 1970s, the field of education began to expand into an emphasis on multiple ways of knowing and learning. This resulted in a paradigm shift that was coined the "reconceptualization of curriculum studies" (Pinar et al., 1995, p. 186). One of the strongest features of this movement was that the emphasis became more on the personal sense-making aspects of curriculum as "understanding, not curriculum development" (Pinar et al., 1995, p. 213). With the emphasis on personal understanding as opposed to standardization of knowledge, a new wave of scholars sought to find their voice.

One of the scholars that emerged out of the second wave of the reconceptualization is William Reynolds (1989). By building on the work of Ricoeur (1981), Reynolds explored new ways of reading both literary and theoretical texts that "posit possible worlds in which the self can be clarified, where the reader might dwell" (Pinar et al., p. 425). He concluded this study by emphasizing the value of metaphoric language to empower the field of curriculum theory to find its own voice. He refers to the work of Connelly and Clandinin (1988), two of the major voices in another branch of the reconceptualization that would place strong emphasis on the use of metaphor in narrative inquiry. These men suggest that "there is no better way to study curriculum than to study ourselves" (p. 31).

This use of metaphor in self-discovery is very evident in the work of one of Connelly's colleagues, Ming Fang He (2003). In her account of the struggle of three Chinese women teachers to find and maintain their identities in the culture of the North American academy, she relied heavily on the "flowing quality of the river metaphor" (p. 129). Because the Chinese language and culture are strongly metaphoric, she found a natural transition in using metaphor to articulate her journey of "personal and professional identity development and knowledge transformation in our acculturation and enculturation processes in China and Canada" (He, 2003, p. 130).

Her writing demonstrates the power of Heidegger's statement that "language is the house of Being" (1947, p. 217). In the midst of all the outward changes in circumstances, metaphor can provide a source of an abiding personal connection to the self and the way it relates to the world and others. If this is true for teachers, it certainly must also be made a reality for those whom we teach.

Metaphor: Imagination's Language in Three Dimensions

Our personal inner landscape depends on metaphor to make connections and enable expression of every variety. Metaphor is a personal pitcher that allows us to draw from the vibrant and freshly flowing river of imagination so we can meet our own thirst for understanding and give expression to others around us. Metaphor is the language of the imagination in times-three dimensions of past, the here and now and the anticipated future. These dimensions are not separate and distinct; they all interact together through personalized metaphoric connections.

Through the generative capacity of metaphor, we are able to unite with our history in ways that enable us to find personal meaning from the past. In the present, metaphor gives articulation to imagination by uniting personal schema with present experience "through its disclosure of patterns, relationships, shadows and lights and slivers of sound that are wholly unexpected, 'new' in some wonderful fashion" (Greene, 2001, p. 154). Metaphor enables us to name our walls and sense gaps in the present. We will look closely at a number of examples of this in the next chapter.

Metaphor draws from the past and present to create a vision of the anticipated future. Through the metaphoric intersecting of these dimensions, we can name our hopes and express our anticipated outcomes for both the near and far-reaching future. Both the critical and creative aspects that are involved in this process as metaphor help us see the union of origin and destiny. At the beginning of the American invasion of Iraq in 2003, for example, I viewed the situation through the "chick inside the shell" metaphor. Everyone knows that the chick must peck its own way out of the shell or there simply will not be much of a future for it. By the same metaphor, I can clearly see that my youngest child, William, as he passionately engages in self-inquiry in the field of linguistics through his *own interests and initiative,* will have a significant future in this field "outside the shell."

In closing this chapter, I return to the two metaphorical trees mentioned in this review, trees that are still very much present with us today. The Cartesian tree now seeks a friendlier façade through means such as the *Race to the Top* Initiative (U.S. Department of Education, 2009). In this current form, the tree gets continually measured and pruned into a standardized concept of growth through pre-established norms and benchmarks written in language with homogeny of meaning. Sadly, this tree is still the most popular because, like so much of our standardized culture, it is a known quantity.

The Vico tree may not be as popular, but it is infinitely more full, vibrant, and creatively defiant of categorical analysis. It is embraced by those who instinctively and experientially know that there is so much more to personal discovery and ways of understanding, being, and teaching than that which can be compared statistically or reduced to the literal flat world of Newspeak. It is my hope that there can be at least some form of a new wave of evolutionary self-adjustment in our culture when once again, those who have been marginalized and ill-defined by standardization will stand up and say, "That is enough." A friend of mine told me that his son was weaned from the bottle in one day. He looked at the wonderful food his parents were eating, stood up in his high chair, and threw his bottle on the kitchen floor and said, "No more bottle!" This is a fitting metaphor because milk is the product of another mammal's digestion. There are so many young people today who want firsthand knowledge in seeing, discovering, and understanding. It is our job as educators to facilitate these personal awakenings, as Maxine Greene calls them. I complete this chapter with an excellent verse from the Wallace Stevens (1954) poem, "Six Significant Landscapes" because it so stunningly expresses the use of metaphor in its highest mode.

> Not all the knives of the lamp-posts,
> Nor the chisels of the long streets,
> Nor the mallets of the domes And high towers,
> Can carve What one star can carve,
> Shining through the grape-leaves.

4

Sensing Gaps

*The search is what anyone would undertake if he were not sunk
in the everydayness of his own life. To become aware of the possibility of the search
is to be onto something. Not to be onto something is to be in despair.*
—Percy, 1979, p. 13

Problem Posing Education and Sensing Incompleteness

Maxine: There is such dynamic power in sensing incompleteness,
Paulo. You have said much in your work about how much more
there is for us to see. I think that recognizing this is:

> where the imagination enters in, as the felt possibility of looking
> beyond the boundary where the backyard ends or the road narrows,
> diminishing out of sight. For a parallel, think of the way the lanes
> and roadways in Constable or Chardin landscapes evoke a viewer's
> imaginative leaps. These paths are promises about where we might
> reach if we tried, if we kept, for instance, moving our pencils or tap-
> ping our word processor keys. Consciousness, I suggest, is in part
> defined by the way it always reaches beyond itself toward fullness
> and a completeness that can never be attained. If it were attained,

A Curriculum of Imagination in an Era of Standardization, pages 43–67
Copyright © 2013 by Information Age Publishing
43

there would be a stoppage, a petrification. There would be no need of a quest. (Greene, 1995, p. 26)

Paulo: Absolutely! That is the essence of focused critical conscious-ness or intentionality as some might call it. This "reaching out" that you describe expresses itself as a question or a problem. The banking method of education provides ready-made and static "answers."

> Problem-posing education affirms men as beings in the process of *becoming*—as unfinished, uncompleted beings in and with a likewise unfinished reality. Indeed, in contrast to other animals who are un-finished, but not historical, men know themselves to be unfinished; they are aware of their incompletion. In this incompletion and this awareness lie the very roots of education as an exclusively human manifestation. The unfinished character of men and the transfor-mational character of reality necessitate that education be an ongo-ing activity. Education is thus constantly remade in the praxis. In or-der to be, it must become. "Duration" (in the Bergsonian meaning of the word) is found in the interplay of the opposites: *permanence* and *change*. The banking method emphasizes permanence and be-comes reactionary; problem-posing education—which accepts nei-ther a "well-behaved" present nor a predetermined future—roots itself in the dynamic present and becomes revolutionary. (Freire, 1970, p. 84)

Maxine: Yes! Moving into the dynamic present is a . . .

> matter of transcending the given, of entering a field of possibilities. We are moved to do that, however, only when we become aware of rifts, gaps in what we think of as reality. . . . It requires imagination to be conscious of them, to find our own lived worlds lacking because of them. (Greene, p. 110)

Imagination and Personal Voice

My quest toward a curriculum of imagination has beckoned me into a ter-rain of incredible variety. The outward spectrum of inquiry and discovery is as vast as the inward "landscapes of learning" (Greene, 1978) that lie within the hearts of the inquirers. The desires and inner capacities of each individual implore them into places where both questions and solutions are treated with equal importance.

At the same time, we heed the astute observation of Greene's work given to us by William Schubert: "Greene has drawn upon both Dewey and existentialists in her work, while being careful not to blend pragmatist problem-solving with the existentialist perception of the need to take responsibility within insoluble ambiguity and discord" (2009, p. 73).

In this chapter, I will explore the role of the imagination in revealing both the answerable and the unanswerable. Both ends of personal inquiry exist in the individual interior language of the inquirer. In my discussion of the role of the imagination in sensing gaps (Henle, 1986), I will give an overview of these various modes of inner language and suggest how they can lead to the creation of personal voice in both public and private domains.

The goal of education is to inspire students for their own journey of personal discovery. One of the greatest gifts that teachers impart to their students is to help them articulate their own questions. This dynamic can awaken the imagination to carry the student out of "bland conventionality and indifference so characteristic of our time" (Greene, 1978, p. 42). This indifference is a further commentary on the debilitating effects of Freire's notion of banking education. He says that it "anaesthetizes and inhibits creative power, [whereas] problem-posing education involves a constant unveiling of reality. The former attempts to maintain the *submersion* of consciousness; the latter strives for the *emergence* of consciousness and *critical intervention* in reality" (1970, p. 81).

Now more than ever, student curiosity and inquiry need to be cultivated to such a degree that scripted learning and assigned roles become as useless as training wheels on a bicycle when you already know how to move forward and maintain equilibrium. It is both sobering and awe-inspiring to think that the questions that lie yet unformed in today's students will determine the degree of discovery and innovation for future generations!

The initial conditions for releasing personal meaning emerge out of a sense that something is missing. These phenomena of "sensing gaps" can take many forms. James (1890) described this gap as being "intensely active.... [A] sort of wraith of a name is in it, beckoning us in a given direction" (p. 251). Identifying and describing this gap often goes beyond the process of recall and into the domain the imagination.

Furthermore, this beckoning of the unanswered leads each individual to make personal connections through subconscious and/or conscious metaphoric expression. This may happen over microseconds or decades. It may take further experience with both external and internal sources to more fully define the shape of the gap. The split-second experience can happen in a "blink" (Gladwell, 2005). However, gaps like the one sensed by Einstein drew him into an intense seven-year quest that yielded the "theory of relativity as its solution" (Henle, 1986, p. 175).

The gap-sensing experience does not exist in a vacuum. Questions come out of knowledge, and the more you know, the more you realize that there is to know. In the same book that is quoted above, Henle enumerates several reasons that gaps are sensed in our experience. These include "contradictions of all kinds" (1986, p. 176) as well as "unexpected similarities" (p. 178). Sensing gaps also occurs "when we encounter strange, unusual, striking, or new phenomena" (p. 179). Henle also mentions "difficulties arising out of the formal characteristics of prevailing theories" (p. 181) as a source as well. Kuhn (1962) would describe this as the possible beginning of a paradigm shift. Think Copernicus, Einstein, and Rosa Parks, for example, as well as those that Greene describes who are "made to feel distrustful of their own voices, their own ways of making sense, yet they are not provided alternatives that allow them to tell their stories or ground new learning in what they already know" (1995, p. 110). At this point, it would be helpful to look more closely at these sources of sensing gaps through applications and experiences.

A Caring Teacher's Experience of Sensing Contradiction

In her wonderful book, *The Inner World of the Immigrant Child,* Christina Igoa (1995) relays a gap she sensed in the form of a contradiction in one of her students that led both student and teacher into life-changing encounter with a curriculum of imagination. At the time, she was the director of a center for refugee children in Hayward, California. In the following passage, she relays the story of Dennis, a 12-year-old student from China.

> Dennis was clearly Chinese, but his name, Dennis, confused me—it didn't fit him. I knew he had come from the Hunan Province of Mainland China, which had been under the domination of Chairman Mao for many years. Both his parents had been doctors in China, but now his father carried crates in San Francisco's Chinatown for a living. The other Asian students in the school were from Hong Kong and Vietnam and Dennis didn't connect with these children. Gently, I gave Dennis a paper and pencil and gestured to him to write his name in Chinese. If could help him feel at home, I thought, and show him that I appreciated and valued who he was as a person, including his Chineseness, perhaps he would relax and allow me to teach him. Picking up the pencil obediently, Dennis began to form some lines, but abruptly he pushed the pencil away and shook his head with an emphatic "No!" At that moment, he revealed to me the energy and force inside him. He acted out the lack of connection between us that still was unable to find expression in words. Silence. (Igoa, 1995, p. 13)

Christina allowed Dennis to work in a quiet part of the classroom until he was ready to choose to break his silence on his own. She also discovered that he liked to create stories with accompanying pictures on blank film strips. Gradually the theme of his stories went from being alone to including others. She also noticed that in story form, Dennis was creating metaphoric action to rid himself of opposing forces. For example, in a second story, he was being pursued by a tiger with yellow eyes and found a place of refuge in a house where a woman was baking cookies (most likely this is a metaphor for Christina's classroom). "After, a man came home. We said to the man, 'We saw a tiger near the mountain.' At night time, the man saw the tiger. He shot the tiger and the tiger was dead" (Igoa, 1995, p. 28). At this point in Dennis's life, he begins to socialize more and become more expressive and confident in his school work. In a final filmstrip story, Dennis himself acts to intervene by shutting the door on a pursuing wolf. Christina continues her narrative.

Dennis's final filmstrip still contained the elements of fear and safety that characterized his previous filmstrips, but a new maturity was also evident. His voice was strong and confident, conveying a "thank you" to everyone. Even more significant was the fact that for the first time in the two years I had been working with Dennis, his name appeared in Chinese. This was indeed a change, a triumph for us all. When he asked me to view his story before he presented it to his classmates, I could not help but notice the Chinese characters on the second frame. I said nothing, although I noticed how he looked at me from the side; but I let the film move on to the next frame as I had done with the others. Silence. I contained the exuberance I felt.

The Wolf
by Dennis
One day, I was flying a kite in the field.
I ran so fast and the kite flew up.
Then I went down the hill to look.
And I saw a wolf coming after me. I was very scared. *(sound)*
Then I ran very fast from the wolf. I ran and ran and ran. *(running sounds)*
Then I ran down the hill.
And I saw a house. I was running to the house. *(running sounds)*
Then I shut the door. *(bang)*
The wolf scratched the door. I closed the door very hard.
After, I heard something coming.
Then, I heard the gun sound. *(bang)*
After, I opened the door
And I said to the man, "Thank you for helping me."
I was very happy and I ran home.
The End.
Thank everybody.

Not long after the "man got the wolf" with a "gun sound," Dennis showed his new found happiness "and ran home." Perhaps he was at home with himself. I saw him at the art table quietly decorating what I thought was a design. He was enhancing it with glue and glitter. It attracted my attention, so I looked over his shoulder. I asked what it might be and he responded in a slightly defensive manner, "My name." Most important was finding ways for Dennis to express his feelings and finding in this filmstrip he reveals his true name, for the first time, writing Qiu Liang in Chinese characters alongside his American name. One week before his graduation to high school, I arrived to find a beautifully designed poster with a message in two languages. In English, it said "Dennis is Alive." The Chinese characters said "Qiu Liang is full of energy and curiosity." With the opportunity to feel safe and cared for at the center, his true self had emerged. (pp. 30–33)

Some may argue that the above story is reading too much into a 12-year-old narrative and that the whole thing is a bit too Freudian for them. But for me it perfectly illustrates Freire's notion of personal metaphor leading to action and personal agency and to Greene's suggestion that allowing students to tell their own story may enable them to come out of the margins by creating vital connections to self-empowering identity. This is a further example of the power of metaphor as the language of imagination to create spaces for living, acting, and discovering out of Heidegger's notion of language as a "house of being" (1947, p. 217), as we noted in the previous chapter in the case of Ming Fang He and her similar search for identity.

Musical Grammar and Imagination

The composer Leonard Bernstein discovered "unexpected similarities" between the structure of music and the field of linguistics. In the lecture series titled *The Unanswered Question* that was videotaped and transcribed at Harvard in 1976; he relates the formation of a question that began in 1937 while he was a student at Harvard. The possible creation of an answer came over 20 years later when he was introduced to the notion of the deep structure of language and generative grammar that is mostly identified by Chomsky's work.

Bernstein sensed this gap while listening to Aaron Copland's *Piano Variations* (1932), through which he made a startling discovery that the first four notes provided a foundation for many compositions that span the whole spectrum of musical history and cultural variety. Through this experience, he began a search for "some deep primal reason for a worldwide inborn musical grammar" (Bernstein, 1976, p. 7). After his exposure to Chomsky's work over 20 years later, he was finally able to articulate the gap he sensed in the form of a question while acknowledging that after so long a time, the notion of music as "the universal language of mankind" had become a cliché. In lecture one, Bernstein wondered if "by building analogies between musical and linguistic procedures couldn't that cliché be debunked, confirmed or at least clarified?" (Bernstein, 1976, p. 10). Imagination was at work to "bring severed parts together" in a completely new and creative way of looking at both language and music.

Parallels between music and grammar became more defined as Bernstein imagined himself as a hominid infant forming his first phonemes. He looked for substantive universals in language to confirm his theory as he worked through the steps of an infant crying for food. He discovered that "ma" or a close derivative was used almost universally across language groups. It seems plausible that a sustained "ma" could be the first "morpheme rewritten as a pitch event" (Bernstein, 1976, p. 15). In other words, perhaps the first musical note ever sounded can be traced to a sustained cry for mother. As he develops his "posed problem" (Freire, 1970), he equates a note to a phoneme, a musical motive to a noun phrase, rhythm functions to a verb, a chord to a modifier, and finally, an essay to a musical composition.

The gap that Bernstein sensed here is not only illustrative of the work in the Freire's problem-posing process; the implications for curriculum are very powerful! If music parallels language in terms of grammatical structure, then it is capable of providing a portal for the enhancement of language to a very high degree. As such, we cannot afford to ignore or exclude the modality of music from the learning process any more than the modality of numeracy. One more point needs to be made before I move to another illustration of sensing gaps.

Bernstein mentions how his Harvard mentor, David Krull, had a lasting impact on his thinking by encouraging him in his quest for musical universals. One of the greatest aspects of teaching is helping students to "wide-awakeness" (Greene, 1978, p. 42) by teaching them to notice features beyond the ordinary. For me personally, all of Greene's body of work has opened me to notice features in works of art, poetry, literature, and philosophy that I probably would not have noticed on my own. Yet out of her personal renderings of works that have helped her find her own personal places in which to dwell, my own eyes and ears have been attuned to new possibilities and ways of seeing and being in the world.

The relationship between Bernstein and his mentor further illustrates the creation of what Freire called "epistemological curiosity" (1998, p. 37.) This is often one of the most neglected areas in schools today and yet it lies at the center of education and personal agency. Helping students to name their questions while modeling the kind of curiosity and enthusiasm for discovering the undiscovered should be central to every classroom and home in the world.

During Bernstein's lectures, he repeatedly illustrated his points by playing pieces on the piano. He also had the entire Boston Symphony play certain pieces. This was interspersed with his very enthusiastic underlining commentary. The effect was contagious. Our enthusiasm for any content area can serve to open doors to personal inquiry by helping others notice connections or "unexpected similarities" that otherwise might simply be passed over or forgotten.

Jackson and the Philosophic Method

The next source of gap sensing that Henle mentioned has to do with encountering "strange, unusual, striking or new phenomena" (1986, p. 179). The examples to draw from here are endless. I am reminded of an incident in the writing of the Dewey scholar, Phillip Jackson. In his work called *John Dewey and the Philosopher's Task* (2002), he meticulously chronicles the evolution of Dewey's concept of "experience" and the nature of philosophic inquiry in general, as exhibited by the four revisions over the space of 25 years to Dewey's (1925/1958) book, *Experience and Nature*. Jackson's research was focused on what might have motivated Dewey to change this text three times, including the removal of "philosophic method" from the title and replacing it with the word "nature," and in his last revision, replacing "nature" with "culture."

The search to discover why speaks volumes about Dewey's commitment to a lifestyle of reflective openness and growth that kept him on a quest in this one particular area for over a quarter of a century. By the same token, for Jackson to care enough about the subject to carefully contemplate these revisions while using his imagination to infer Dewey's motivation suggests more than an emotionally detached word study.

Wittingly or unwittingly, as Jackson's own philosophic urge carries him forward, he reveals his own disequilibrium in understanding (p. 96). In Chapter 4, he selects some of Dewey's poetry to illustrate Dewey's sense of "being adrift" (p. 74) at times in pursuit of pure empiricism. Throughout Jackson's inquiry, he cites Dewey's use of nautical and map-making metaphors to describe the task of the philosopher (pp. 59, 70–76). He concludes this section by observing that, for Dewey, "certainty and uncertainty coexist every step of the way" (p. 76). Does this also include Jackson's own view?

At the conclusion of this inquiry, it appears that Jackson becomes more of what he sees and admires in Dewey as they both pass through the fog of ambiguity and move further away from philosophy as a method to philosophy as a means of finding "alternate ways of conceptualizing various aspects of the whole (the 'gross phenomenon') of living the philosophic life" (p. 94). The case is never really brought to closure for either Dewey or Jackson. There is enough evidence to suggest that Dewey was slowly drifting away from orthodox scientific method toward a more humanistic approach to inquiry. Jackson sees Dewey's substitution of the word "culture" for "experience" (p. 97) in his unfinished last manuscript of the text as a signifier that perhaps Dewey was moving away from hard science to "some of the more humanistically inclined disciplines" (p. 96). Still, no one is left with a sense of confirmation beyond reasonable doubt. "As Greene observes, 'conclusions [are] thrillingly left incomplete'" (Jackson, 2002, back cover).

Perhaps the gap was never meant to be closed by either Dewey or Jackson. The immense significance I find in both Dewey's example and Jackson's pursuit of its implications is that they exemplify the intrinsic values that are needed to live and teach a curriculum of imagination. When a tree stops growing, it is dead, even though it may take decades for the shell of the tree to finally rot away. Yet living trees, just by "being" can provide direction and act as landmarks to those who have lost their way. Freire strikes this note very strongly with his narrative concerning the change/permanence dialectic.

> Problem-posing education affirms men and women as beings the process of becoming—as unfinished, uncompleted beings in and with a likewise unfinished reality. Indeed, in contrast to other animals who are unfinished, but not historical, people know themselves to be unfinished; they are aware of their incompletion. In this incompletion and this awareness lie the very roots of education as an human manifestation. The unfinished character of human beings and the transformational character of reality necessitate that education be an ongoing activity. Education is thus constantly remade in the praxis. In order to be, it must become. (1970, p. 84)

This notion also resonates deeply in all of Greene's work when she says, even in her 90s, "I am who I am not yet" (quoted in Pinar, 1998, p. 1). In summary, Jackson's posed problem led him to emulate Dewey's example of a lifestyle of reflection and growth, and as such, this example illustrates for us that a curriculum of imagination is never complete, static, or permanent, but is always in the making.

Curriculum Emerging From the Gaps

The last source of gap sensing that Henle mentions comes from "difficulties arising out of the formal characteristics of prevailing theories" (1986, p. 181). This gap can lead to discoveries as far reaching as the Copernican revolution or to a radical change in what is perceived as the purpose of field of curriculum studies. In both cases, conventional knowledge barred the door to whole universes of personal discovery. In the case of Copernicus, this was quite literal and involved outer space. In the field of curriculum, in the late 1960s, sensing gaps spawned a movement away from lock-step planning and scripted textbooks into an emphasis of curriculum as so much more than methodology.

More specifically, I am referring to what has been termed "Reconceptualization" of the field of curriculum. Pinar et al. (1995) observed that "by the early 1970s, the field was up for grabs" (p. 187). A full-blown paradigm shift occurred in the 1970s with the Reconceptualization, a term that was coined by Pinar (1975) in *Curriculum Theorizing: The Reconceptualists*.

At the core of this shift was the notion that *understanding* curriculum was vastly more important than *developing* curriculum. Indeed, the very nature of curriculum study shifted from *doing* curriculum to curriculum as *being*. With this paradigm shift came the notion that curriculum theory should change how both teachers and students think, and the journey of self-discovery became its own reward.

The groundbreaking work by Pinar and Grumet (1976), called "Toward a Poor Curriculum: Introduction to the Theory and Practice of Currere," provided a model for both teachers and students to explore their own inner landscape through autobiography, with a view toward self-actualization. Although this work was not widely received in the field initially, by 1991, it was clear that "currere" became one of the major thrusts in the reconceptualized field of curriculum studies (Pinar et al., 1995). Through the regressive phase of currere, the writer is enabled to reconnect with the past in modes of "self-shattering, revelation, confession, and reconfiguration." In the progressive phase, the writer engages in a "kind of free-associative 'futuring' during which one seeks one's fantasies of what one might be. These imaginings are expressions of who one is not now, of *material felt to be missing* [emphasis added], sought after, aspired to . . . they are a means by which we midwife what is not yet born" (Pinar, 2004, p. 55). Both phases rely on the work of the imagination to make life history connections and then carry ourselves outward and upward to new spaces of being.

Another area suggested to me by Bill Schubert is what he refers to a "plants growing in cracks" metaphor (personal communication, 8/21/11). Imagination operates in the "in-between" of overly defined categories. Sometimes in nature, the life force in a seed can even split rocks! Follow this link for a picture that is worth a thousand words: http://www.emporia. edu/earthsci/outreach/ckft.html

The image is accompanied by this text: "This sandstone concretion was split by tree growth! Notice the small rock to the left of the boulder. The tree grew into and through a fracture, breaking the concretion over time" (Driessen & Morales, 2000). Maxine Greene's words come to mind immediately:

> [I] was demeaned in my early days of college teaching by being told I was too 'literary' to do philosophy. That seemed to mean that they thought I was ill-equipped to do the sort of detached and rigorous analysis of language games and that for a long time dominated the academic world. (Greene, 1995, p. 113)

Indeed the tree of her imagination split the concrete of Cartesian male-dominated rigor with such dynamic force that educational philosophy was forever altered as a result.

Metaphor and Naming Gaps

The concept of currere is very strongly connected to the work of the imagination and the use of metaphor. Our personal inner language depends of the imagination to make connections and enable expression. Egan (1992) concisely describes the work of the imagination by saying that "imagination lies at a kind of crux where perception, memory, idea generation, emotion, metaphor, and no doubt other labeled features of our lives, intersect and interact" (p. 3). In fact, the imagination is the intersection itself.

Pinar's contribution to this concept can be traced to an article that he wrote called "Working from Within" (1972). This piece is built on the metaphor of teacher as painter who draws on inner sources of the imagination in the creative process of expression. He expresses this by saying, "Like some modern painters, my students and I have come to feel that we rarely need to refer to subject matter outside ourselves. We work from a different source, we work from within" (Pinar, 1972, p. 331). Quite often, inward connections are made through the use of metaphor. Currere itself is a metaphoric term that comes from the "Latin infinitive form of 'curriculum' meaning: to run the course" (Pinar & Grumet, 1976, p. vii). As such, it is a metaphor for one's life journey.

In all four of these examples of gap sensing, metaphoric expression is used as a means to name the problem and initiate a process of personal discovery. Taken together, we have seen, in the case of Dennis, the wolf metaphor resulting in breaking the contradiction of identity; music as language; mapmaking and sailing as the philosopher's task; and curriculum as personal life journey. Through metaphor, personal experience connects with new concepts in a way that can expand understanding.

Lakoff and Johnson (1980/2003) describe abstract concepts as having "a literal core but... extended by metaphors, often by many mutually inconsistent metaphors. Abstract concepts are not complete without metaphors. For example, love is not love without metaphors of magic, attraction, madness, union, nurturance and so on" (p. 272). This extension carries inquiry beyond the problem-finding stage and into new discovery. I hesitate to describe this process as linear. Discovery can go back and forth, in and out, and in limitless directions in order to make personal connections. Dewey (1934) observes, "The constant adjustment of both the new and the old *is* imagination" (p. 272). This adjustment comes from within the learner, not from the material being learned. As I explain in the next section, this constant adjustment is accomplished through the unique faculties of each of its participants. The features of the language of thought are as varied as the visible features of each person on this planet. As I continue my journey toward a curriculum of the imagination, I will describe how these languages of the mind are used by the imagination in the incubation "phase" of discovery.

Incubation

Mostly everyone has had the experience of breaking through obstacles in problem solving after a short time of retreat and rumination of the difficulty. It may be anything from a plumbing problem, writer's block, or coming to resolution in the theory of relativity, as in the case of Einstein. Obviously, some concepts need more applied contemplation than others. There are some characteristics of problem solving that are common to all humans and certainly should be considered in a curriculum of imagination.

Modell (2003) suggests that "what makes us uniquely human is an unconscious metaphoric process. Unconscious autobiographical memory, the memory of the self and its intentions, is constantly recontextualized, and the link between conscious experience and unconscious memory is provided by metaphor" (p. 25). As we observed in the last chapter, metaphor is not just a fanciful rhetorical device. Lakoff and Johnson (1980/2003) posit that "metaphor is a neural phenomenon" (p. 256). Neural networks are created in the brain by the combination of subconscious memory and experience through metaphoric connections. Consequently, metaphor is a tangible, physiological connector of the subconscious and conscious, the new and old, and the mental and physical through means of visual, verbal, somatic, and auditory concepts. Modell affirms this notion when he says that "metaphor formation is intrinsically multimodal, as it must engage visual, auditory and kinesthetic inputs" (2003, p. 32). It is during the incubation phase of problem solving that new connections are formed.

In order for these networks to be established, time for reflection is essential. For example, the act of writing this book has provided me with many episodes of metacognitive reflection. This has taken on many forms. Sometimes I was aware of a breakthrough in thinking while in a half dream state of sleep. Many things came together while mowing the lawn, or walking, or on my frequent bike rides. I was delighted to read examples of the creative process of many people that confirmed all these many modes of incubation time. The mathematicians Changeux and Connes (1995) give an excellent summary of the incubation process that is worth noting here. The process begins with focused conscious intention followed by a period of setting this direct concentration aside. There must be a time allowance for germination or incubation. Often an unexpected solution will make itself known. This is followed up with a time of critical assessment. During this period, connections are formed through each person's unique internal metaphoric expression.

The Heart of Imaginative Curriculum

One of the salient aspects of this inquiry has been the discovery of many examples of nonverbal metaphor during the creative process. Of course, in order for these instances to be shared, there is a need to expressly articulate these concepts into verbal expression of some kind. This notion brings me right to the heart of my quest for a curriculum of imagination. Personal voice begins with internalized, metaphoric connections and finds articulation through multiple discourses (Moffett, 1968) including numeracy, drama, music, dance, graphic and fine art, literature, craftsmanship, invention, agriculture, technology, athletics, and all forms of communication. Students need time to reflect in the same ways that the great creative minds used in these examples did. Some were visual thinkers; some thought best while moving; some of them needed to constantly touch the objects of inquiry. Meanwhile, back in a city not far from where I live, there is new playground equipment donated to the school but still in the box because recess has been cut out in order to give more time to test preparation!

Visual Imagination

Visual thinking is one of the foremost sources of creativity and yet it is also one of the most neglected in schools today. After considering the history of imagination and metaphor, it is clear that the reason for this is that it is much harder to standardize mental images. Yet it is clear that they play a role in the discovery process of every content area. One of the classic examples of this is from the mathematical/scientific domain in the life of Albert Einstein. He came to resolution about the theory of relativity by picturing himself riding through space on a light wave while "looking" back at the wave next to him. I think we would be hard put to find someone else in history who could claim a similar experience with those images. Apparently, Einstein only saw the need to think in words in a secondary stage after working out his concepts in a way that he could reproduce them at any time. Here is what he wrote about this notion in a letter to the mathematician Hadamard (1945):

> The words or the language, as they are written or spoken, do not seem to play any role in my mechanism of thought. The psychical entities which seem to serve as elements in thought are certain signs and more or less clear images which can be "voluntarily" reproduced and combined. There is, of course, a certain connection between those elements and relevant logical concepts. It is also clear that the desire to arrive finally at logically connected concepts is the emotional basis of this rather vague play with the above-mentioned elements. But taken from a psychological viewpoint, this combinatory play seems to be the essential feature in productive thought—before there is any connection with logical construction and words or other kinds of signs which can be communicated to others. The above-mentioned elements are, in any case, some of visual and some of muscular types. Conventional words or other signs have to be sought laboriously only in a secondary stage, when the mentioned associative play is sufficiently established and can be reproduced at will. (pp. 142–143)

The cultivation of the transference of visual metaphor to written language is one that has been sadly neglected because we are still coming out of the impact of behaviorism, which had little use for interior phenomena. It has been through the lens of Gestalt psychology that the imagistic thought has received greater credibility. In the writings of this field of study, "thought and sight are dynamically interconnected" (John-Steiner, 1985, p. 85). John-Steiner goes on to say that visual thinking has advantages over some aspects of verbal thinking because the former has more fluidity and therefore it yields a "great diversity of graphic and plastic means used by creative individuals in shaping and communicating their inner visual notions" (1985, p. 86). As a whole, we are not harnessing these advantages in schools because expression of this variety is harder to control and assess. Breakthroughs of comprehension and discovery across every content area might very well created by the cultivation of imagistic imagination provided by the domain of the arts.

Kinesthetic Imagination

The house I live in has a yard area of at least five acres and a lot of grass has been cut while incubating this chapter. On one of the days, I hit a half brick that was hidden in some weeds that had grown up around an azalea bush. Needless to say, the blade was destroyed. I tipped the mower on its side and tried to loosen the retaining bolt with just a socket wrench. It would not budge. I found a longer piece of pipe to put over the end of the wrench, and it still stayed immovable. Finally, the nut broke loose as I used a large chunk of concrete to hold the blade in place while I torqued down on my makeshift extended wrench handle. Through this entire operation, I was aware of how unified my fingers and brain worked together in solving this simple problem. I became aware in a new way that I could "think" with my fingers as I intuitively thought about what would or would not work in this situation. I thought of my brother-in-law, who can diagnose problems in a car engine by touching the small end of his longest screwdriver to the cylinder heads, one at a time, and putting his ear on the other end. Of course there are computers that can handle this whole operation now, but mechanics still engage in thinking with their fingers and ears literally hundreds of times every day while they work on cars for lawyers and English professors and artists and politicians.

On a recent trip to North Carolina, I talked to a young man named Jason who dives in the muddy waters of the Dismal Swamp region, with hopes of finding Civil War artifacts. Obviously, there is nearly zero visibility when one is completely submersed in mud. Jason has to rely completely on the sense of touch. As he finds submersed objects, he runs his fingers across the surfaces and his fingers send a "flash message" to his brain. He can tell whether a bottle is antique or not by checking it for asymmetry, which would indicate that it was hand-blown glass. He reported with great enthusiasm how much fun it is to try and ascertain the identity of unknown or unfamiliar objects through the sense of touch alone.

How fortunate Jason is to have a father who cultivated this unusual capacity in him as they engaged in this activity together. There are millions of students in our schools today who are forced to sit for hours at a time and passively take in someone else's words. And for those who cannot sit still, we have lots of drugs, and if that does not work, there are "alternative schools" or the "vocational track." Yet in many countries outside of North America, the lines between hands-on learning and academic subjects are very blurred or nonexistent.

Auditory Imagination

My wife has called me a "flypaper brain" all through our marriage. I attribute this to being an auditory thinker. In fact, I do retain spoken language much better than written language. This notion led Coreil (2003) to question visually driven approaches to teaching English. Here is an account of breakthrough that came out of a "sensed gap" in his English teaching experience in Saudi Arabia:

> *"These guys cannot learn English,"* the Brit said. *"We have suggested dismissal, but the headmaster says no. Good luck and don't send any of them to my office, none, no matter what!"* So I went into the classroom, clicked my heels and said, "Hi! I'm Clyde." I drew not a smile. Forgetting what I had prepared, I proceeded to read them a simple story. They seemed to quiet down. So I read it again and again each time, I asked simple questions about the story, and a couple of students blurted out very short and barely understandable but generally correct answers. Their *ears* had been working far better than their *tongues.* Anyway, later that afternoon, I recorded a couple of stories and copied the tapes one by one on my recorder. Then I wrote ten true false questions about the story. At the end of class next day, I handed out the tapes and exercises and gave them three days to finish. I did not include the printed version of the tape scripts.
>
> After the three days, they had completed the assignment but were grumpy and implied that it was far too difficult . . . but asked where was the next one. They were even more upset when I said there was no next one, but that I would make another that afternoon and have it ready in a couple of days. If I hadn't, I fear that my motorcycle tires would have been sliced by a curved dagger. They weren't lazy. But many of them had grown up on the desert. They were fiercely independent and hated normal English class because it involved for them humiliation, embarrassment and frustration. On the other hand, the listening work was difficult, but they could do it. And they needed something they could be proud of.
>
> It was incredible to me how well they mimicked my tape-recorded voice: *"Oh, no,"* Ali said. *"I can't go back there!"* I could hear traces of my Cajun accent

in their voices. That class learned a lot of intonation, pronunciation and even grammar with me hardly ever mentioning it with my raspy voice. I am in no way a professional reader. I made up for this deficiency by hamming it up unashamedly and doing some slightly questionable things myself. For instance, I would pause occasionally and—breaking the narration—sternly say something like, "Abdul, wake up! This is not a tent!" Subsequently, in middle of class, one or another of them would repeat one of those admonitions in exactly the tone of voice I had used. So it wasn't only targeted speech production that they learned, it was a number of aspects of speech patterns that I wasn't even aware that I had, much less had put on tape. I became more aware than ever of the great, extremely subtle interpretive powers of the human ear. If I had given them the printed tape script instead of the tapes, I don't think I would even remember the class now. Again, there's something very special about the human voice, the human ear, and the human imagination, and I am afraid that we are neglecting all three in many of our classrooms.

Numerical Imagination and Critical Literacy

There are those in our schools whose inner language is numerical. In the movie *Rain Man* (Johnson & Levinson, 1988), Dustin Hoffman gives a superb performance as an autistic savant that is based on the life of Kim Peek. Here is a little information about the real Rain Man:

> Kim did not walk until age four. At that time he was also obsessed with numbers and arithmetic, reading telephone directories and adding columns of telephone numbers. He enjoyed totaling the numbers on automobile license plates as well. Since 1969 Kim has worked at a day workshop for adults with disabilities. Without the aid of calculators or adding machines, he has prepared information from work sheets for payroll checks. (Treffert, 2006, n.p.)

The existence of people like Kim Peek suggests that there is a distinct inner language of numeracy. In fact, Einstein further stated in his letter to Hadamard that he expressed himself "in a different language, I think in mathematics" (Hadamard, 1945, p. 45). In my work as a literacy teacher, I have witnessed many students who did well in math computation, but not so well in reading comprehension. One reason for this is because many of the word problems are removed from the context of real life outside of schools.

Gutstein (2006) is working to remedy this situation by combining the language of math with issues of social justice. As a student of Michael Apple, he was strongly exposed to Freire's work and others in the concept of critical consciousness. As a math teacher, he sought for ways to apply these concepts. He accomplishes this through problem-posing projects such as studying the mortgage loan rejection rate ratios by ethnicity in a number of U.S. cities. Another interesting project involves the cost of a B-2 bomber, "$44,754,000,000 for 21 planes" (p. 246) compared to the cost of college tuition.

After the students compute the cost per bomber compared to the cost of tuition at a state university in Wisconsin, they compare these figures. Next, he has them write their opinion of this situation and then write how they feel about doing math in this way (p. 247). With projects such as these that transcend overly guarded walls between disciplines, Gutstein's work is a step in the right direction.

Verbal Imagination

None of these kinds of thinking exists in isolation. Ideally, they can all work together as they shape and are shaped and by one another. One of the recurring themes throughout this inquiry is that each of these multiple literacies can lead to the discovery of personal identity and agency by serving as portals to enhanced reading and writing. Language is communication; as such, it serves as a "bridge between individuals who wish to overcome divisions born of the diversity of human experience. It is also a bridge between inner thought and shared understanding: the past and the present, the world of the senses and the realm of thought" (John-Steiner, 1985, p. 111).

With this notion, I am taken back to my own methodology in writing this book because the act of writing on this topic is motivated by my own quest for sense making and the discovery of personal voice. Thinking evolves into communication in the process of writing as it passes over the bridge of inner thought to shared understanding that John-Steiner mentions. I love what the literary figure Arthur Miller had to say about this:

> For myself it has never been possible to generate the energy to write and complete a play if I know in advance everything it signifies and all it will contain. The very impulse to write, I think, springs from an inner chaos crying for order, for meaning, and meaning must be discovered in the process of writing or the work lies dead as it is finished. (1960, p. 275)

Since communication is central to all content areas of schooling, verbal thinking is also vitally important. However, the bridge between inner thought and communication is not located on a one-way street. Multiple literacies work in both directions in order to facilitate problem finding and resolution. They serve as entry points for personalized construction of meaning as well as mediums of expression in communicating with others.

One of the clearest examples of the role of imagination in both these directions is found in Gallas's (2003) work. She describes how students take on the meaning of text and read it from the "inside out" through identity, discourse acquisition, and authoring. The results of this may offer a way out of the ongoing debate between phonics instruction versus whole language approaches.

The Language Ego

Linguists often speak of the power of the language ego. This phenomenon involves the ability to take on the identity of a speaker of any language or dialect. This not only includes target vocabulary and syntax of a language. It also includes gestures and the learner's perceptions of the attitude of the language. An excellent example of this is seen in Jamie Foxx's Oscar-winning portrayal of Ray Charles in the film, *Ray* (Benjamin & Hakford, 2004). Anyone who has ever heard the real Ray Charles in dialogue or performance would be strongly aware of the excellent job Foxx did of becoming the text of his life. To prepare for his role in the movie, he actually went to a school for the blind, in order to learn how to read Braille.

In language acquisition, there is an unpredictable point when communication becomes part of the subconscious. Anyone who has studied a foreign language intensely is aware that when you begin to think or dream in that language, you are on your way to fluency. By far, the best method of language learning is in the context of real communication, not in the isolation and recitation of specific points of sentence-level grammatical items. *Literacy involves imaginative connections to text, speech inflections, gesturing, and the ability to "read" a person's intent.*

Reading From the Inside Out

The great debate between phonics vs. whole language instruction continues. The National Reading Panel endorses a strong emphasis on phonics, or bottom-up processing. Others continue to emphasize the role of context in top-down processing. Gallas's view of inside-out learning presents a view that is outside this dichotomy. In actuality, both these models are implicit in the inside-out approach.

Identity Stage

In the identity stage, the learner takes on the prescribed role of the text. For example, when a student is reading a text from science, through the process of identification, he or she can emulate the role of a scientist by adopting the speech and mannerisms of a scientist, thereby "reading" the text from the "inside out." Gallas quotes from Lave and Wenger in this connection. They write, "Learning involves the construction of identities" (in Gallas, 2003, p. 70).

This theory came alive for her as she took her students on a field trip to a science museum. As four of her students stood next to a display of dinosaur bones, they began to pretend they were scientists. They adopted what they perceived to be the speech and appropriate tone of scientists in their role-play.

She further supported this position from her own childhood experience. She remembered learning about measurements when she was a child with a toy oven. She sums up this identity stage by saying that "first the child takes on the role of a scientist: second, the student takes on the point of view of the object or text under study" (p. 74). Of course, this is not limited to the field of science. It could be history or math or preparing a meal or building a kayak.

This stage works well with adult learners also. One of the first classes in which I received an A was Cultural Anthropology in my sophomore year of college. This class was great for hyperactive boys. The class room contained a rich collection of artifacts that the award-winning professor had collected over his tenure at a small community college. Many of these were hands-on exhibits of Native American tools and pottery from nearby excavations in the Finger Lakes regions of upstate New York. We actually conducted excavations of our own during the semester. Consequently, this class was one of my favorites out of all my undergraduate studies. By "reading" the text of this class with our bodies in real life exploration, everything about it became alive.

Discourse Acquisition

The next stage that Gallas presents is discourse acquisition. This stage takes identity several steps further. What is involved here is the appropriation of the identity through what she calls a "tool kit" (p. 86) of a discourse. This consists of the language, tools, text, and forms of inquiry that are discipline-specific and used to master an identity.

This is accomplished through "hands-on" application. For example, if a student is reading about how to make a drum from a hollow log, he or she can learn the text inside-out by making the drum and then learning to play it. She succinctly sums up this stage in saying that "the tools and texts of a subject gain their vitality when they are brought into *productive* contact with a student's experience" (p.87). This involves mental, emotional, and somatic productivity. Standardized tests measure perhaps only one tool in this kit: information about the topic.

This brings to mind an adult English language learner that I taught during the 1998–1999 school year. He had been a welder in Bosnia and had come to upstate New York as a refugee along with his wife and daughter. I sought to teach him to read in English through traditional methods, including phonics. This helped somewhat because he needed to familiarize himself with sound/symbol correlations. He was one of the hardest working students I had ever taught. In spite of this, there came a point of blockage in fluency until we decided to try a "discourse acquisition" approach.

I found a book on welding processes that he was already familiar with from his work in Bosnia. I would copy pages with diagrams and other visually descriptive content. This made a huge difference for him, not only in the content of welding procedures, but in general language acquisition as well. I wonder what would have happened if I had stuck with the "required competencies" curriculum for English language learners.

Motivation is intrinsic when self-actualization, through identity, is strengthened. When students see that they are the text, confidence increases, and affective barriers are overcome. This is so important today because the gap between the "haves" and the "have nots" continues to widen as a result of standardization. Test scores measure test-taking ability. Real assessment has to do with students demonstrating what they know through identification, discourse acquisition, and, finally, a presentation of that knowledge in another form. That brings me to the last part of Gallas's theory.

Authoring

The final stage of this process Gallas calls "authoring." This needs to be distinguished from the internal aspects of processing language by a public act of presenting it in another form, for a real audience. This can accomplished through a musical performance or dance, writing, solving an equation, drawing or painting, storytelling, drama, or repairing a car. This stage requires a demonstration of text in a way that can be validated by others through the recreation of meaning. She succinctly states this through her observation that "literacy is a process of merging who we believe we are with what we show we can do" (2003, p. 100).

This concept is very much in keeping with the philosophy of John Dewey. For him, nothing was ever learned until there was an application of some kind in the dimension of becoming the text. Anytime there is a separation of principle from application, he observed that principles become "fossilized and rigid; they lose their inherent vitality, their self-impelling power" (1910/1933, p. 213). No wonder there are so many high school drop-outs in our country today. The drudgery of processing information without transforming it through personalized application has sucked the life out of the most fascinating of topics.

Yet, at the same time, no one wants to turn teenagers loose to drive cars without giving them the full opportunity to become the text of the driver's manual. This is because there is an immediate danger to everyone if all it took to get a driver's license was a satisfactory score on a multiple-choice test. All teaching and learning should carry this same kind of weight. There is just as much danger for our culture to measure student achievement on standardized tests scores alone!

Some students learn how to play the test game and can get by without ever being inspired to become a text. Littky and Grabelle (2002) observed that one of his 15-year-old students had only finished reading one entire book in her life, and yet she consistently received either an A or B on her entire transcript. Littky and Grabelle explain:

> She had never finished a book because she didn't have to. She got good grades regardless. If she needed to write a book report, she saw the movie or read the first and last chapters and that was enough. Lori put as much effort into reading as her teachers did in evaluating her reading. They didn't see what she was missing and she didn't tell them. (p. 156)

Perhaps this is why some students refuse to apply themselves at all. They see through the grading game and conclude that it is another example of being treated as an "it." Meanwhile, many of these same students may prove to be exceptionally bright if given the opportunity to "author" what they have learned, as Gallas and Dewey suggest. In fact, they will, more than likely demonstrate a deeper knowledge of the text because it has been processed from the inside out.

In contrast to regurgitating facts on multiple-choice tests, Gardner's (1999) definition of intelligence supports this applied approach to learning. He defines it "as a biopsychological potential to process information that can be activated in a cultural setting to solve problems or create products that are of value in a culture" (pp. 33–34).

Whether it is sensing gaps, problem finding and problem solving, or critically examining the results, learning moves in all directions and is never static or two-dimensional. No one would want to be invited to your home for dinner, only to find a recipe for shrimp scampi, along with a multiple-choice quiz on the text taped to the plate. Eating is believing!

Sensing Gaps, Incubation and Political Change

Gaps awakened by critical imagination are both personal and social and often political in the process of resisting predefined answers and status quo thinking. Sometimes the political implications of sensing and discovering gaps may not be directly understood by the discoverer. For example, Einstein had no way of knowing that his view of relative time and space would help to shatter the paradigm of modernism. Neither did Bernstein fully understand what implications his view of musical grammar would have on the demise of behaviorism. Igoa's (1995) work has become part of an entire movement to advocate for the immigrant child and the marginalized native who needs help in finding his or her own voice. Changes of any kind begin with sensed gaps, and questions can open universes of discovery far more effectively than impersonal and irrelevant answers.

Consider the chain reaction sensed gaps can release when they spark others to question and make personal choices that lead to social change. The great Civil Rights movement in America provides a salient example because there was so much going on behind the scenes in individuals and small groups for decades before the massive marches, sit-ins, bus and business boycotts, and voter registration drives took place.

Most people credit Rosa Parks as the "mother of the Civil Rights movement" and she certainly was a major link in the chain, but six months before she was arrested, she had been to Myles Horton's Highlander School for a civil rights seminar and one of her teachers was Septima Clark (Charron, 2009; Horton & Freire, 1990). During her visit, she was strengthened to act because "she found respect as a black person and found white people she could trust" (Horton & Freire, 1990, p. 153). However, it was not just Myles Horton who helped fan the flame that led Rosa to act. Consider what she said in an interview with Cynthia Stokes Brown:

> I noticed [at Highlander in 1954] how Septima Clark could organize and hold things together in this very informal setting of interracial living. I had to admire this great woman. I was just the opposite. I was tense, and I was nervous, and I was upset most of the time. . . . I felt that I had been destroyed long ago. But I had the hope that young people could be benefited by equal education. (Parks, cited in Seeger & Reiser, 1989, p. 25)

By the time this meeting took place, Septima Clark had already been actively engaged in teaching for social justice for over 30 years (Charron, 2009). So on that eventful day in December of 1955 when Parks refused to give up her seat to a White person, there is little doubt that the "sensed gap of the unjust" had been incubating in her being for many months. Her action led to arrest, which served to awaken thousands to the gap she sensed. A young minister named Dr. Martin Luther King was one of them. The Montgomery Alabama bus boycott ensued. This movement sparked nationwide change, including the motivation of thousands of college students to teach Blacks how to read and write, with the stated goal of preparing them to participate in voting and the democratic process. Yet the Citizen School Curriculum they used can be traced back to Septima Clark, who taught adult literacy classes to natives of St. Johns Island, South Carolina and other areas of the state, starting in the 1920s. This vision and purpose of these classes was to prepare Blacks to pass voter registration exams as well as basic life skills such as using bank services and signing other forms. This work prepared Clark to develop a "citizenship pedagogy in the mid-'50s while working for the Highlander Folk School" (Charron, 2009, p. 2). The responsibility of this work was transferred to the Southern Leadership Conference after Highlander was forced to close and through this group with Septima Clark still in supervision along with many others, "the teachers collectively taught more the twenty five thousand people" (ibid. p. 3).

This work in the United States is very similar to what Freire would later call "critical consciousness" (1974) in his work in citizenship education in Brazil. In this context, Freire distinguishes between action and free will as integration and adaptation when he says that "integration results from the capacity to adapt oneself to reality *plus* the critical capacity to make choices and transform that reality" (p. 4). In contrast, Freire defines adaptation as a dehumanizing response that is "at most a weak form of self-defense. If man is incapable of changing reality, he adjusts himself instead" (1974, p. 4).

In the context of the Jim Crow south of the early 20th century, to be critically conscious meant moving beyond Booker T. Washington's vision of servile adaptation through basic literacy and vocational schools to one of directly challenging practices of segregation and other forms of racial injustice. Freire would go on to be one of the most widely quoted and influential educators in recent history while Clark, who was doing very similar work, remained in relative obscurity as she made a way through the uncharted waters of inequality of the early 20th century and into the perilous storm of the great Civil Rights movement.

I close this chapter with the astute summary quoted from Maxine Greene: It is "only through the projection of a better social order that we can *perceive the gaps* in what exists and try to transform and repair. I would like to think that this can happen in classrooms, in corridors, in school-yards, in the streets around" (2008, p. 111, emphasis added).

Me too, Maxine, me too!

5

Toward Empathic Imagination

The extent to which the self can enter into the other can be seen
as an expression of the freedom of the imagination.
—Modell, 2003, p. 117

Paulo: I think we need to focus more on the dialogical aspect of
imagination by emphasizing the vital importance of the role that
it plays in empathy, which in turn, makes dialogue possible. Any
theory of imagination that does not convey a connection to the
personal stories of others is suspect. It seems to me that the very
opposite of imagination is viewing others through the predefined
frameworks of essentialist and socially constructed categories. We
are not predisposed to think like this. It is a social construction.

> The perversity of racism is not inherent to the nature of human
> beings. We are not racist; we become racist just as we may stop be-
> ing that way. The problem I have with racist people is not the color
> of their skin, but rather the color of their ideology. (Freire, 1997,
> pp. 85–86)

Maxine: I especially appreciate what you said about the connection between imagination and empathy. Racism looks at people in the abstract. Empathy enables us to see, know, and relate to people in the personal present.

> Imagination is what enables us to cross the empty spaces between ourselves and those we teachers have called "other" over the years. If those others are willing to give us clues, we can look in some manner through a stranger's eye and hear through their ears. That is because, of all our cognitive capacities, imagination is the one that permits us to give credence to alternative realities. It allows us to break with the taken for granted, to set aside familiar distinctions and definitions. (Greene, 1995, p. 3)
>
> In this regard, I have learned the value of connective details. "Without them, it is extraordinarily difficult to overcome abstraction in dealing with other people. A fearful oversimplification takes over in the blankness; we see only [Russia], [student movement] [ethnic minorities]" (Greene, 1995, p. 95).

Paulo: Exactly! This "oversimplification" often takes the form of rigid definition or essentialism. That reminds me of something that the great 20th century philosopher, Emmanuel Levinas, said: "The more we define the other, we are able to do violence to the other" (1998, p. 9). This certainly has been confirmed by history both before and after the holocaust!

Maxine: Absolutely. The road to dehumanization commences with labeling by categories. For me, one of the greatest antidotes to this kind of thinking has been found in reading literature. The lived experience revealed in personal story emerges in my own "consciousness, and by so doing, transforms it, as social scientific accounts, or even psychological ones would never do" (Greene, 1995, p. 4). Literature always carries the "potential to subvert dualism and reductionism, to make abstract generations questionable" (p. 96). I love what Barbara Kingsolver said in *Newsweek* a while ago, about the power of fiction.

> Fiction creates empathy, and empathy is the antidote to meanness of spirit. Nonfiction can tell you about the plight of working people, of single mothers, but in a novel you become the character; touch what she touches, struggle with her self-doubt. Then when you go back to your own life, something inside you has maybe shifted a little. (quoted in Shapiro, 1993, p. 61)}

Paulo: I have experienced that shift many times. I think we can be critically conscious, even in the reading of fiction, because the thing that makes a story really work is that it elicits a response of shared human experience, and as we said before, for the reader who is critically conscious—or wide awake, as you say—the walls between the objective and the subjective worlds are obsolete.

The Essentialism/Relativism Dichotomy

Every human is unique. Each one is the product of his or her own biological and cultural journey, with unique schemata and capacity for personal and public ways of knowing and being and self-expression. Both essentialism and extreme relativism miss the mark insofar as offering an adequate representation of personal signature and voice. When applied to identity, essentialism refers to "the notion that individual groups have an immutable and discoverable 'essence'—a basic, unvariable, and presocial nature" (Moya & Hames-Garcia, 2000, p. 7.). The most obvious examples are categories of race, class, and gender. The concept of ethnicity breaks things down further, but still comes short of a full account of individual difference and personal story.

Extreme relativism, on the other hand, treats biological differences as a socially constructed myth and personal identity as a fluid concept. As we saw in the last chapter, the inner landscape of each human is as varied as his or her outward physical features and is the result of both genetic and cultural influences. It is through the power of personal story that we are able to move out of the essentialist/relativist dichotomy and into the domain where each individual path of experience is incomparable and immeasurable in one aspect, but also universal in terms of sharing human life.

In my experience, any time I am impressed by any form of either positive or negative action or expression or way of thinking, I always want to know the story of the person behind it. This desire covers the complete spectrum of human experiences and identities, ranging from Gandhi to Hitler or from Serena Williams to one of the indigenous tribes of Papua New Guinea, for whom treacherous betrayal is a virtue. It also includes people as diverse as Alice Walker, Stephen Hawking, Joni Mitchell, Theodore Kaczynski, Atticus Finch, or Sauron. I concur completely with Greene's (1995) notion about the act of reading fiction (or any personal narrative) when she says that it "reveals to me my stake in the human condition, helping me reach the ground of my being which is also the ground of learning, of reaching beyond where one is" (Greene, 1995, p. 93). If we are critically conscious, we will see ourselves in the story of others, which in turn enables us to see beyond external abstractions of humanity into the lived experience of others. Of course, we may not always like what we see, but without self-reflection, empathy is impossible.

Another problem that occurs within the essentialist/relativist dichotomy is that it often presents a sanitized version of historical events and viewpoints that avoids paradoxes in false binaries. This view of history "shuns half tints and complexities; it is prone to reduce the river of human occurrences to conflicts, and the conflicts to duels—we and they... winners and losers... the good guys and the bad guys, respectively because the good must prevail otherwise the world would be subverted" (Levi, 1988, pp. 36–37).

For example, there is a persisting mistake that slavery in America was only a problem in the southern states. In his book *Black Bondage in the North*, Edgar McManus (2001) challenges this fallacy.

> Slaveholding reflected social as well as economic standing, for in colonial times servants and retainers were visible symbols of rank and distinction. The leading families of Massachusetts and Connecticut used slaves as domestic servants, and in Rhode Island, no prominent household was complete without a large staff of black retainers. New York's rural gentry regarded the possession of black coachmen and footmen as an unmistakable sign of social standing. In Boston, Philadelphia, and New York the mercantile elite kept retinues of household slaves. Their example was followed by tradesmen and small retailers until most houses of substance had at least one or two domestics. (p. 41)

Even after slavery was abolished in the Northern states, there was often a persistent attitude of racism. In *Democracy in America*, De Tocqueville observed that "race prejudice seems stronger in those states that have abolished slavery than in those where it still exists" (1844/1966, p. 243).

In a more positive light, especially during the present wave of Holocaust-denying propaganda that comes from a wide array of sources, a Near East studies scholar named Robert Satloff spent four years searching and researching for an "Arab Oskar Schindler." This is an excerpt of an interview with Satloff on the PBS News Hour conducted by Margaret Warner (2006):

Margaret: What are a couple of your—I hate to say favorites—but your nominees for an Arab Oskar Schindler?

Robert: Well, I suppose my top nominee is a Tunisian gentleman named Khaled Abdelwahhab, who was in a small seaside town named Mahdia in Tunisia. And he learned one evening that a German officer was going to rape a blonde, beautiful, blue-eyed Jewish woman. And he knew that family of the Jewish woman, and he got there first. And he knocked on the door where she and her family were seeking refuge. And he said, "You have to come with me." And he ferried all of them in his car for the rest of the evening back and forth, because there were several families in the same place, ferried them to a farm that he and his family had outside town. And he kept them there for six weeks until the end of the war. And that, to me, is true heroism.

Margaret: All right. Give us another.

Robert: Then, even in the heart of Europe, right under the eyes of the Nazis, in Paris, there's a fantastic story about a man named Si Kaddour Benghabrit, who was the rector of the mosque of Paris, the imam of the largest mosque of Paris. And there's compelling evidence that he saved up to 100 Jews in a very clever way. He gave them certificates of Muslim identity, birth certificates, marriage certificates, so they could pass as Muslims and thereby avoid arrest and deportation.

Margaret: Now, how did the descendents of these people react when you tracked them down?

Robert: The response to these wonderful stories of humanitarianism itself was very complex. Many times, I would come to the homes of the sons and daughters or grandchildren, and they were not delighted to learn about the heroic deeds of their grandparents. And as one of them told me with great candor, "Look, what my father or grandfather did half a century ago was one thing, but politics has intruded, and I'm not too excited to hear about this stuff these days." And to me, that's very sad that it's become almost toxic in many parts of the Middle East to remember that there was a moment when some Arabs saved some Jews.

Fragmentation and Personal Story

One of the aspects of a curriculum of imagination that needs increased cultivation has to do with the removal of well-guarded walls between genres and content area subject matter and between fiction and nonfiction. The influence of Carlyle's (1859) great man theory in history is slow to die, but the hunger to know personally and locally is increasing. Carlyle's theory looks at history from the top down, through the lens of the most prominent figures in history as the source of causation. Meanwhile, the stories of those who have provided the ballast to the ship of human progress in everyday life have quite often been ignored. I think that is one reason for the interest in "reality" television. It is clear that much of it is contrived, but, at the same time, its popularity gives us an indication that there is now a greater interest in the lived stories of everyday people.

The World Wide Web has opened the gates to daily deluges of more information than we could ever possibly need on any given subject. This may be one factor in the increase of the hunger for personal connection. Journalists such as Malcolm Gladwell, the author of *The Tipping Point* (2002) and *Blink* (2005), are selling millions of books because they are written in a personal narrative style of prose that makes the stories of real people and events come alive. By the same token, Tom Wolfe's first work of fiction, the *Bonfire of the Vanities* (1987), is a stunningly accurate and yet satirical treatment of life in the New York City during the 1980s. The ability to capture the nuances of dialogue, sights, sounds, and smells, as well as the zeitgeist of that period, from this master journalist, served to strengthen a new movement in literature.

All these observations underline for me the need to imaginatively create spaces beyond the walls of the fragmentation of knowledge. The stories of individual lived experience that combine valuable content with personal, sensory-laden literary prose can tie geography, history, literacy skills, math, and science with the arts in ways that give context and humanness to dead and isolated facts.

Cultivating Critical Multiculturalism

Being White is an entitlement, not to preferred racial attributes, but to a raceless subjectivity. That is, being White becomes the invisible norm for how the dominant culture measures its own civility (McLaren, 1991).

Multiculturalism has become a buzzword in education. Reclaiming what this word is supposed to signify cannot be accomplished by coming up with a new buzzword. The only way to ever truly reconstruct any concept is through a lifestyle of demonstration or praxis of the very words that have lost their potency because of miseducative examples. Nieto (2000) says that multicultural education must be more than "tacos on Tuesday." Such practices do little to challenge the assumptions of White normalcy. We hear the expression "I see no color" quite frequently. In this expression, racism is still conspicuous by its absence. True multiculturalism not only sees color, it celebrates the rich variety of experience and culture across the entire family of man.

Sleeter (1993) offers a very potent metaphor for watered-down multiculturalism as a bulletin board, by relating the comments of her interview of teachers to find out how they construct race:

Whiteness was taken as the norm, as natural. When teachers told me about "multicultural lessons" or "multicultural bulletin boards," what they usually drew my attention to was the flat representations of people of color that had been added. Multidimensional representations of whiteness throughout the school were treated as a neutral background not requiring comment. (p. 166)

The demographics of the United States are rapidly changing. If the fallacy of Whiteness as the "normal" background is to be kept in place, it will require an even greater propagation of historical and cultural "White lies" than what already exist in the present. According to the United States Census Bureau's projected statistics, by 2050, the percentage of the population under the designation "White alone, not Hispanic" will be 50.1% (USA.org, 2011).

Apple (2001) points out that "race as a category is usually applied to 'nonwhite' peoples. White people are usually not seen and named. They are centered as the human norm. 'Others' are raced" (p.209). Everyone is "other" to someone. The fallacy of a racial norm of any kind must be a vital and ongoing part of a curriculum of imagination, and one of the best ways to approach this is through personal stories.

I am reminded of a time I was walking with friends, on the streets of Ocho Rios, Jamaica, and found myself on the receiving end of racial joking. A man was laughing and pointing at me while he said, "White mon, white mon, where are your eyebrows?" It was funny in one way, but I admit, it did not feel that pleasant at the time, and that was just a few minutes out of my entire life!

Dehumanization by Labeling

In one of Ayers' works (2006), there is an account of a study that was conducted "within a few square blocks of a poor neighborhood on Chicago's South Side" (p. 93). The study revealed:

No less than 28 distinct ways—and didn't claim that she had covered the entire territory—in which people described themselves as single mothers: living with grandparents, living with boyfriend, living with aunt, living with best friend and her child, living with same-sex partner, sister and sister's husband living next door and helping out, mother living around the corner, child's father paying rent, and on and on. A few felt abandoned by men, a few others liberated from them; some were doing well, others not so well; a few had adopted children or were their legal guardians, and one said, "I chose to be a mother without a life-partner—I'm single by choice." The variety is dazzling, the scope and range and specific meaning-making seemingly endless. . . . The complex reality is, of course swept away with the lazy label "single mother": the tough edges are all sanded off, the differences homogenized and stuffed into a simple gray bag. It is difficult to see this when the blinders are applied—in this case, hidden in the policing language of social science. (pp. 93–94)

One of the most rewarding teaching experiences I have ever had took place when I was teaching adult literacy with a "single parent." I will call her Latoya. She showed up in my class on a Monday morning with an irritable and closed manner. The local office for public assistance had given her a seven-month window to prepare for the GED exam.

I could see that she was a hard-working student right away. Every day, a little more of her guard came down. By Thursday I said to her that she wouldn't need to use up all her benefit time preparing for the test. I told her that she would be ready in three weeks, not seven months. Gradually, she let her story out.

She had been in an abusive relationship with a man. One day, he beat her up for the last time. She literally picked his sofa up and threw it out of her trailer, along with all his other belongings. After that, she rode a bicycle eighteen miles to sign up for public assistance. A few days later, they had sent her to my classroom. She wanted to become a veterinary assistant. I kept assuring her that she would do well in that position because she loved animals so much. By the end of two weeks, her demeanor was a lot less caustic. Just before she left to take the GED exam, I assured her once again that she would do quite well on it. She said something that really struck me as one of the most important aspects of being a teacher. She said, "Mr. Lake, you are the only person in the world who believes in me now." The weight of that statement floored me! In many cases, teachers may provide the only care and nurture that some students receive.

Geneva Gay (2000) writes that teachers must have an "unequivocal faith in the human dignity and intellectual capabilities of their students. They view learning as having intellectual, academic, personal, social, ethical, and political dimensions, all of which are developed in concert with one another" (p. 44). This can only happen when teachers become far better at reading hearts than they are at reading labels.

Curriculum as Conversation

In his provocative and refreshingly clear work, Sidorkin (2002) posits a theory of evil as the "absence of relation, an inability or unwillingness to relate to another human being. Evil is objectifying the other, taking an utterly monological stance toward the other" (p. 186). The concept of evil as the objectification of humanity cuts through much of the dogma about ethics and morality. We have already seen, in a previous chapter, that "dark imagination" operates in the domain of objectification. One of the central themes in all of Freire's work is that the way unjust power is maintained is through seeing others as "object" (1970). This is certainly true in education as well as in the thousands of criminal acts that are committed against others every day.

The ability to listen to people requires imagination because, by it, we are opened to the polyphonic aspect of meaning, not just the narrow sounds of cliché or the kind of inward thoughts that cause knee-jerk reactions to what we hear. The prejudiced person is only in tune with himself. Curriculum as conversation "is a matter of attunement, an auditory rather than visual conception, in which the sound of music (for Aoki, jazz specifically) being improvised is an apt example" (Pinar, 2004, p. 189). Curriculum as conversation (Applebee, 1996) can serve to tune the ear to participate, to resonate with the voice of others. This is no scripted endeavor, but like the jazz analogy, there is a certain aspect of the spontaneous that is welcomed. In the shared dimensions of spontaneous dialogue, there is a fuller experience of knowing. Freire is very strong on dialogue as a shared way of knowing: "I engage in dialogue because I recognize the social and not merely the individualistic character of the process of knowing" (1993, p. 379). Dialogue, however, is much more than rearranging the chairs in the classroom. Genuine dialogue is not the product of preformulated questions and responses. In Freire's view (1970), dialogue must be open-ended. Again, the imagination is called upon in ways that enable us to reach beyond our own thoughts and patterns of thinking.

Sidorkin (2002) offers further insight into the nature of curriculum as conversation, saying that relations cannot be described by one person's perspective: "Relation in general is possible only in the presence of difference. Totally identical entities cannot relate to each other. Relations result from plurality, from some tension born of difference" (p. 98). This difference is not something that needs to be overcome by a "fifty/fifty split." Every voice needs to be heard, not lowered to the least common denominator.

Sidorkin goes on to say that one of the greatest needs in schools is the cultivation of curriculum as conversation by focusing on the

> ability to "read" relationships to reflect on these cases, to talk and write about relationships. The key skill here is the ability to reconstruct the other voice. A teacher must develop this ability to hear what has not been said, to formulate what his students are not able to articulate, to engage in a dia-

logue when the other party may not be willing or ready to engage. The ability to understand human relations relies heavily on the heightened ability to hear and respond without preconceived notions of truth. (p. 100)

This ability to read relationships will carry over into all content areas. In fact, our praxis becomes more relevant, and potent, to the degree that we are in tune with the voice of others. In English teaching, for example, Michael T. Moore shares the notion that grammar errors are really thinking errors. "These errors are caused by faulty thinking. Generally, I label this as writing with oneself in mind as an audience. When you write for any audience one must take care of the thinking that elicits communication" (personal communication, May 2005). This notion covers many aspects of curriculum theory because language is central to both learning and communication. Imagination can provide insight into the ways language is *perceived or received* by others.

Exploratory Drama and the "Other"

The ability to read relationships is very important in teaching because, without it, we would not be able to sense whether the students are really grasping what needs to be taught. In the language of the last chapter, curriculum as conversation enables both teacher and student to "sense gaps" in personal connection to content. This was the experience of Tonya Perry (2005). In a very well-written narrative style, she discusses her experience of using exploratory drama to enhance the personal connection to the reading of *Anne Frank: The Diary of a Young Girl* to a high school class. She observed a marked difference between the ability to recall facts about the text and the students' ability to comprehend it. Through the use of exploratory drama, she was able to increase empathetic comprehension. She focused on the lines in the text that referred to the periods of silence in the attic that Anne Frank's family had to practice.

> Instead of reading the play the next day, I asked the students to enter the room without talking. As they sat, I told them they were all hiding from the Nazi forces like Anne Frank. Immediately, without any additional description, I showed them video clips of what we would face if anyone discovered our whereabouts. We quietly watched images of soldiers looking for the Jewish people in their homes and taking them to ghettos. As time progressed, we watched trains fill with people heading to concentration camps. Images of families separating and deplorable living conditions occurred more frequently. Students silently transitioned to the large taped square in the middle of the floor. I asked them to sit quietly for five minutes without talking

and think about what we would face if we or someone else talked, placing our lives in grave danger. (p. 122)

This exercise proved to be effective in increasing comprehension by taking vicarious meaning making to a higher level. Perry summed up the value of this exercise by pointing out that "authentic drama assignments capture the students' ability to understand complex concepts and use them in multiple contexts" (p. 122). What struck me the most about this classroom experience is that the students read the text with great phonetic facility but still lacked the context that was needed to truly feel, see, touch, and understand the story. It took imagination to transcend walls between 21st-century students in Alabama and the scene inside an attic in Nazi-occupied Amsterdam in 1942. I understand the limitations as well. There is no method to fully convey the sheer terror that this family experienced. At the same time, critical literacy can enable us to look through the cracked door into the lives of others, and exploratory drama is engaged literacy that involves reading with your body.

Imagining the Lives of Others through Cross Cultural Dialogue

Through the advancements brought in by technology, social imagination can be released to shatter stereotypes on a global scale. One of the most powerful uses of live digital satellite communications I have ever witnessed was in the form of a cross-cultural dialogue between four American and four Jordanian high school students on a program that was aired on San Francisco's *World Link TV.* The four Americans were from Lowell High School in San Francisco, and the four Jordanians were from the Arab National School in Amman, Jordan. About 900 students at Lowell and more than 1,000 in Amman watched a recording of the event and then discussed their reflections and reactions. The director of the *World Link* network recalls the event:

> [It was] a unique meeting of cultures, hearts and minds. Four young Americans, two girls and two boys, meet electronically with their counterparts from an Arab culture perceived as hostile to ours. The conversation ranges from political disagreements through cultural stereotypes and misperceptions, interracial dating, drugs, the Intifada, teen suicide bombers, Martin Luther King, the bias of the media, and U.S. support for Israel. Although they agree on much, they remain worlds apart on issues like suicide bombings. Since most of the perpetrators and the victims of suicide bombings have been young people, it is fascinating and inspiring to see teens from both cultures grappling with this issue. (Spencer & Olsson, 2002)

After the live linked dialogue, the four Arab young people spoke to each other in their native language:

Jahed: Usually Americans don't support us, so it was a surprise that they agreed with us on so much.

Farah: They agreed on everything except suicide bombers...of course, not all Americans are like this...but it changed some of my preconceptions. For example, I thought all young Americans took drugs, but they don't.

The American students also had a follow up discussion:

Hassan: The experience made me feel more like an American, made me realize that I am accountable for my country's actions.

Rene: When I realized that the four of us—Hispanic, Chinese, Jewish and Arab-Americans—were the face of America for them; it made me proud and happy (Spencer & Olsson, 2002, pp. 2–3).

I am sure that the factors of worldwide audiences played a role in determining the responses these young people shared with each other. However, I cannot help but think that the experience did help to break essentialist notions about the unknown "other" in some measure. This approach is certainly in the making, but offers promise for further exploration in dialogue even across sharp political and cultural differences.

Metaphor and Empathy

In her collection of essays called *Metaphor and Memory*, Ozick (1991) shares about her experience of being invited to speak to a group of physicians, "not because I knew anything about disease, but because I knew nothing at all" (p. 264). She had been invited because she was an "imaginer by trade" (p. 266) who might be able to offer suggestions to help the medical profession express more empathy for their patients. At the time she presented her reading, she was not well received. However, a search of journal articles from the field of medicine reveals that, either directly or indirectly, a favorable influence was made upon the healing community by her presentation. Her central thesis is that "metaphor is one of the chief agents of our moral nature" (p. 270) because without it, "we cannot imagine the life of the Other. We cannot imagine what it is like to be someone else. Metaphor is the reciprocal agent, the universalizing force: it makes possible the power to envision the stranger's heart" (p. 279).

Metaphor has the power to bring together both the speaker and the interlocutor in personal history. This can be in real conversation, or in the pages of a novel, or a song, or a metaphoric expression of any kind, including the nonverbal variety, such as dance or gesture. This conjoining of histories can occur at both the conscious and subconscious levels by metaphoric connection. Certainly both metaphoric thoughts and emotions play a major role in this experience, but as we have stated throughout this inquiry, there is a dynamic wholeness to body and mind that should always be considered as one.

Ozick goes onto say this about metaphor and memory: "Metaphor relies on what has been experienced before; it transforms the strange into the familiar" (p. 282). Metaphor provides the ability to resonate with another's history because somehow we recognize our own experience in the experience of the other. In literature, an entire novel can serve as a metaphor. In the foreword to *The Fellowship of the Ring,* for example, Tolkien states, "As for any inner meaning or 'message,' it has in the intention of the author none. It is neither allegorical nor topical. As the story grew it put down roots [into the past] and threw out unexpected branches" (1954). Yet the work itself abounds with universal and personal metaphorical references that any serious reader is able to see immediately. Visual and musical metaphor also has the power to evoke empathic resonance. Both mediums can function as fully as verbal metaphor for some people.

Arnold Modell (2003) says that visual and musical metaphor also has the power to evoke empathic resonance. Both mediums can function as fully as verbal metaphor for some people. Modell cites an astute example of this in a reference to James Breslin (1993), the biographer of the abstract expressionist Mark Rothko. Breslin says that the artist "painted lack, he painted the great vacuum at the center of his being" (p. 280). His paintings convey "a melancholy sense of loss," what he called "their intimations of mortality" (p. 280). Later in Breslin's obituary in the *New York Times,* he is quoted as saying that Rothko's paintings "create an empathic space in which to confront emptiness and loss; they create an environment for mourning" (Thomas, 1996). The personal history of both painter and viewer came together in imagination to create empathy in such a powerful way that, according to the same obituary, Breslin changed his career from English professor to art historian as a result of Rothko's work.

Musical metaphor has always been a very influential part of my inner landscape. This experience includes many different genres, including music with no lyrics. I have been touched deeply by the field hollers of the American slaves and the "disconcerting" chord structures used by Aaron Copeland, as well as ballads of every kind. One story song that struck a deep place in me subconsciously at first is "The Frozen Man" by James Taylor (1991). Here is the first verse:

> Last thing I remember is the freezing cold
> Water reaching up just to swallow me whole
> Ice in the rigging and the howling wind
> Shock to my body as we tumbled in.
> My brothers and the others are lost at sea,
> I alone am returned to tell thee,
> Hidden in ice for a century
> To walk the world again.
> Lord have mercy on the frozen man.

When I first heard this song, it brought tears to my eyes, but I was not fully aware of the reason for it. As I thought about it, I realized that, for James Taylor, perhaps the whole song was a personal metaphor for his "thawing" from a lifestyle of heavy substance abuse. He may have felt that he had missed a very large part of his life during that period. As I heard the song again sometime later, I recognized my source of empathic projection. It was this: I almost died from Legionnaire's disease in 1987. I woke up in a hospital after being unconscious with this strange illness. During my prolonged recovery, I found that I had more empathy for all bedridden patients, but especially those with near respiratory failure. "The Frozen Man" became a very personal metaphor for getting my life back. Modell (2003) says further that "we select objects in current time that will provide the meaning that will enable us to alter the experiences of the past. We invest those objects with feeling when we perceive a metaphoric correspondence between present experiences and unconscious memory" (p. 164). I am certain that this is what happened to me, although as I look back, I can see that perhaps empathic extension began subconsciously.

These two examples illustrate again one of the central themes of this inquiry. Imaginative/metaphoric connections can transport the imaginer beyond walls of every kind into personal spaces of meaning. From the vantage point of the personal, communication through multiple literacies becomes part of the public domain. In the first example, there is Breslin, who is profoundly struck by the art of Mark Rothko, so much so that he writes a moving biography of the artist and changes careers from English professor to art historian. In my own case, a powerful connection was formed with a song that led to understanding in several ways. First of all, I came to know, personally, what it means to experience metaphoric empathy with a work of music. Secondly, I was able to name an area of self that is able to resonate more with those who are afflicted with near respiratory failure, as well as their families. Thirdly, I am able to write and teach about these personal discoveries in ways that will hopefully enable others to notice what otherwise might be ignored. It is our personal story that provides the dynamic of teaching and learning. Our students are more likely to notice ways of knowing for which we are passionate, that generate motivation to move beyond every barrier into spaces of personal and public spaces of being. This reality brings me once again to the empathic center of a curriculum of imagination. It is not a rigid method, but a release from the inarticulate stasis; "it is by writing that I often manage to name alternatives and to open myself to possibilities. This is what I think learning ought to be" (Greene, 1995, p. 107). I return to Ozick's sublime prose on this notion, to close this chapter.

> Through metaphor, the past has the capacity to imagine us, and we it. Through metaphorical concentration, doctors can imagine what it is to be their patients. Those who have no pain can imagine those who suffer. Those at the center can imagine what it is to be outside. The strong can imagine the weak. Illuminated lives can imagine the dark. Poets in their twilight can imagine the borders of stellar fire. We strangers can imagine the familiar hearts of strangers. (1991, p. 183)

6

A Curriculum of Imagination in the Making

Paulo: I want to bring up some things that you wrote in *Dialectic of Freedom*. Just out of curiosity, I counted the number of times you use several words. You refer to "walls" ten times, "obstacles" 24 times, and "barriers" nine times. That is a total of 43 times!

Maxine: I never knew I used those words with such frequency. I guess that is some indication of my passion for freedom. Naming obstacles and then resolving to be your own agent in moving beyond them is a theme that is very dear to both of us. Freedom of imagination *starts* by naming obstacles, yet some people are so "afraid of acknowledging structures, they can scarcely think of breaking through them to create others, to transform" (Greene, 1988, p. 20).

Paulo: Yes—and fear leads to adaptation to life within walls! Freedom is integration, not adaptation. There is a universe of difference between these two conditions.

A Curriculum of Imagination in an Era of Standardization, pages 85–105

> Integration results from the capacity to adapt oneself to reality *plus* the critical capacity to make choices and to transform that reality. To the extent that man loses his ability to make choices and to transform and is subjected to the choices of others, to the extent that his decisions are no longer his own because they result from external prescriptions, he is no longer integrated. Rather, he has adapted. He is "adjusted." ... The integrated person is person as subject. In contrast, the adaptive person is a person as object. (Freire, 1974, p. 4)

All that we have been saying about imagination and generative metaphor, sensing gaps, or naming walls, and then creating spaces with our own words and in dialogue with others leads to personal meaning and empowering freedom.

Maxine: There are so many different kinds of obstacles to name! There are "limitations on free speech, mindlessness, mechanism, routine behaviors, the rule of brute habit—none of which would be noticed by those who were somnolent or who had no wish to move beyond" (Greene, 1988, p. 6).

> But those of us who desire to be wide awake can nurture the same capacity in others by our example and by bringing both obstacles and spaces for personal meaning to the notice of our students. When Dr. Martin Luther King and his associates "came together to name the obstacles," they certainly did not stop there. They chose to take responsibility, to act, to choose a way of being in the world. (Greene, 1988, p. 101)

Every one of us has opportunities daily to name walls and take personal responsibility to envision ourselves beyond them and move into spaces of personal discovery and meaning through choices we make. That has been my personal experience. We must face things as they are before we can envision what might be, then make choices that lead to expanded horizons of being.

Paulo: To be "wide awake," as you say, one must throw off the yoke of determinism and mythical, magical thinking that keeps them from authentic reflection. However, this state "cannot exist apart from action, men must also act to transform" (Freire, 1974, p. 20). Imagination, through critical consciousness, enables the personal naming of walls and creates the hope of moving beyond them. Then, through metaphoric connections, it makes possible the creation of personal meaning.

Maxine: And one aspect of personal meaning is the ability to "see with the stranger's eye and hear with the stranger's ear" in ways that create public dialogue and polyphonic expressions of meaning.

All this is what is meant by imagination and so much more. This is an ongoing, unfinished conversation, Paulo!

Paulo: Absolutely—the work of imagination is never static and always in the making!

Throughout this book I have explored conceptions of imagination and metaphor through an imaginary dialogue between Maxine Greene and Paulo Freire based on their writing and other scholars of aesthetic and critical pedagogy. I have discovered mutual and dialectical themes in their conceptions of imagination and metaphor. I arranged passages with a minimal amount of conversational conjecture in ways that expressed agreement and the tension brought about by evolving paradigms in the sociopolitical, philosophical, and literary views of imagination. These themes include imagination as hope, reflective, generative, and critical imagination, and views of metaphor as shaped by the same paradigm shifts that brought about new ways of looking at imagination.

In order to understand the nature of a curriculum of imagination, I use the principle of contrast, by tracing the history of standardized testing, eugenics, tracking, and overly scripted practices used to present "official knowledge." I have learned more about the connections between standardization and the highly influential impact of capitalism and the business model on the field of education.

In this context, I expand my understanding of Freire's (1970) notion of "problem posing" education and Greene's (1988) concept of "naming walls" by applying Henle's (1986) work on "sensing gaps" to Igoa's (1995) connection to the *Inner World of the Immigrant Child*. Bernstein's (1976) theory of musical grammar, Jackson's (2002) inquiry into Dewey's evolving view of experience, and Pinar's (2004) work in currere. I also discuss the need for an incubation period during which personalized metaphoric connections are made in a variety of multiple forms of literacy and how these inner landscapes are transformed into discourse through identification and authoring.

Furthermore, I seek to understand the role of imagination in communal ways of knowing that take us beyond the continuum of essentialism and relativism through personal story and metaphoric connections into empathic relationships. I challenge the concepts of "Whiteness as the norm," "seeing no color," and "tolerance." I share autobiographical and biographical examples derived from over 15 years of experience in teaching that illustrate the power of metaphor in personal story to create empathy.

Understanding a Curriculum of Imagination Through Four Commonplaces

As I reflect upon what I have learned from this inquiry, I turn to Schwab's (in Westbury & Wilkof, 1978) notion of four commonplaces to envision a curriculum of imagination in the making. Schwab had much to say about the need to open the field to democratic dialogue and forms of inquiry that focused less on "proof," while opening spaces for "discovery and invention [through] pluralities of knowledge" (1978, p. 336). I am intrigued by some of the terminology that Schwab brought to the field of education from his background in biology, because a curriculum of imagination is rich with metaphors of life and nature. I remember that it was Schwab who referred to the field of curriculum as "moribund" (in Pinar et al., 1995, p. 187) by the end of the 1960s. Another potent word he brought from biology is "coalescence" (Schwab, 1978, p. 365), which literally means to grow together in forming new living organisms. Coalescence is an important aspect to understanding Schwab's notion of four commonplaces because they continually grow together in organic oneness, and like every living organism, they overlap in the function. They are only delineated for the sake of inquiry and discussion. The four commonplaces (milieu, teacher, learner, and subject matter) are integral parts of curriculum. Drawing from my observations and developing understandings, I use these four commonplaces to reflect upon the findings that emerged from this inquiry and to imagine what these four commonplaces would look like in a curriculum of imagination in the making.

Imaginative Milieus

Schwab used the term "milieus" (1978, p. 366) to describe the context of learning that included school and classroom environment, community and family, class and ethnicity, as well as values and attitudes that in the learner's environment comprise the "cultural climate" (p. 367). The current curriculum milieus that characterize a standardized curriculum are dehumanizing, abstract, and impersonal, with a focus on individual achievement and singular interpretation and predefined answers and a downward configuration of authority.

To counter the current curriculum milieus, imaginative milieus are comprised of a number of elements that work together to create the environment of problem posing, personal discovery, and shared understanding that are central to a curriculum of imagination. The most vital elements in this commonplace are the milieu of hope; a milieu of shared interests; the milieu of fluid language, incubation, critical consciousness; dialogue across differences; and the sense of belonging and care. I will look briefly at each of these, in connection with what I have already written, as I envision this curriculum in the making.

The one constant feature that I have discovered that is always present in this commonplace is the milieu of hope. This is so much more than the eternal sunshine of passive optimism. Hope is allowed to exist by choice. Of course, the imagination can also take people into the depths of despair if, by it, we come to imagine the worst. But in an educative and personal dimension, I have learned that hope exists because we refuse static representation and given knowledge, while reaching out toward that which is not yet expressed or experienced or created. Hope looks past barriers to learning, labels, and test scores and takes us out of abstraction, into humanizing and personal knowledge of the entire domain of education, society, and culture. I vividly remember being told in the early days of my graduate-level studies that I needed to go on to doctoral studies because I belonged there. I was surprised by this comment at first, but the professor who told me that imparted hope to me in a way that enabled me to persevere through the entire program of study.

Because the field of education has been sequestered behind standardized walls for so long, any hope that is present is often anemic. I have been amazed at the number of people in the field of education who have ceased to reach beyond, either because they were tired of fighting the system, or they had seen too much and given into despair. In 1994, after having suffered so much misunderstanding and injustice, including living in exile, Freire wrote, "Without hope there is little we can do. It will be hard to struggle on, and when we fight as hopeless or despairing persons, our struggle will be suicidal. We shall be beside ourselves, drop our weapons, and throw ourselves into sheer hand-to-hand, purely vindictive, combat" (1994, p. 9).

One of the ways that Maxine Greene renews hope is through literature and the arts. She says that fiction "revealed my stake in the human condition helping me reach the ground of my being—which is also the ground of learning, of reaching beyond where one is" (1995, p. 93). Further, she says that "art offers life; it offers hope, it offers the prospect of discovery" (p. 133). This discovery is not in the structure of art and literature on the surface level. It is because through interaction with these works of creation, there is a nurturing of the spirit of quest. She so eloquently describes this, saying that "if the significance of the arts for growth and inventiveness and problem solving is recognized at last, a desperate stasis may be overcome and hopes may be raised, the hopes of felt possibility" (p. 132). One of the places where hope needs to be generated the most is in the teacher acad-

emy. A curriculum of imagination should include literature and art and poetry and music in ways that make possible an ongoing renewal of the milieu
of hope as personal and social vision. Teacher preparation is so overloaded
with methodology and mandated practices that there is very little space
left to lift out of the stasis of the predefined and two-dimensional at a time
when teachers are in short supply anyway. The lack of cultivation of imagination as hope may be causing many teacher candidates to quit before they
have barely had a chance to start.

In a telephone conversation with Nel Noddings, I asked her what she
did to maintain hopeful imagination. She said, "I work in my garden, hug
my cat, and watch the sun rise over the ocean" (personal communication,
September 4, 2006). She does most of her writing in the winter. I can certainly resonate with her in these details of her life. I have to be outside
almost every day in order to feel fully alive. Nature continually renews itself,
and we can draw from its forces by some variety of continual exposure to
it. In some ways, there is a literal connection between the milieu of hope
and the environment of nature. However, renewal of hope is often a very
personal and individual exercise, out of which we are enabled to maintain
a public vision. The social activist/educator bell hooks returns repeatedly
to the writing and speeches of Dr. Martin Luther King to renew her vision
(hooks, 1994, p. 33). While I was thinking about what various people do
to maintain hope, I talked to Gloria Ladson-Billings because in her presi-
dential address at the 2006 AERA meeting, she explicitly named walls, and
she also rekindled hope. Her presentation was one of the best examples of
imaginative uses of multimedia combined with rich storytelling I had ever
witnessed. She said that what keeps her hope strong is her "personal faith."
She further stated that "just because something is impossible that doesn't
mean you shouldn't do it" (personal communication, September 5, 2006).
She discussed Nelson Mandela's release from prison after 27 years in confinement as an example of hope triumphing over the impossible. Mandela
was able to maintain a climate of hope until the day when he was literally
taken beyond walls. The climate of hope is continually carried by those
who have lived in reach of its enabling power. Students need to be taught
to notice the inward landscape of those whose hope stayed strong in the
face of seemingly insurmountable obstacles. Honest and personal stories
of persistence by inventors, social reformers, writers, artists, musicians, and
athletes and firsthand accounts of the triumph of the marginalized need to
be brought continually into the vision of both teachers and students.

Another milieu is described by He, Phillion, Chan, and Xu (2008) as a
"curriculum of shared interests" (p. 231). This is described in very positive
and hopeful language:

We envision this curriculum of shared interests as one where all members of the school community and policy making milieu have shared common interests. Families connect their concerns about the education of their children with those of the larger society. Schools share their interests in educating immigrant students with families and communities. Individuals have equal opportunities to "take and receive from others" and to have "free interchange of varying modes of life experience" (Dewey, 1916, p. 84) and are willing to adjust their interests to the interests of others in a larger society. In a curriculum of shared interests, teachers cultivate cultural competence to recognize contributions of ethnically and linguistically diverse students. They develop pedagogical competence to enrich the curriculum for immigrant and minority students. Students are encouraged to value their cultural and linguistic heritages, respect and accept difference, critically examine their position in society, and perceive themselves as agents of positive curriculum change. Policy makers and administrators learn the nuances of immigrant students' experience of curriculum. They value the knowledge held by teachers, students, parents, and other curriculum stakeholders and incorporate this knowledge into policy making. Families and communities share responsibility with schools and government organizations to create a school environment that is equitable, safe, and caring. This environment is the ideal milieu for developing a curriculum of shared interests that commits to a high level of achievement, not only for immigrant and minority students, but for all students. (pp. 231–232)

This passage describes an "ideal" environment for a curriculum of imagination in the making. While I am aware this is far from what actually takes place in the present, it is very important to continually cultivate our dreamscape. Just think what inspiring effects Dr. Martin Luther King's speeches had on the listeners, for example. Speaking and cultivating vision is a very powerful aspect of imagination.

In imaginative milieu, there is a shared awareness that "when the same school curriculum is prescribed for all, individual interests and abilities get short shrift and difference is perceived as a deficiency" (Martin, 2002, p. 125). I was able to make personal sense of this concept by looking at my own family.

During this inquiry, I thought about the wide array of interests and capacities that are present in my children and how they might all be called upon to use them in a disaster like a hurricane. My son David, a lineman, would be called on to restore electrical power to the infrastructure, including hospitals. My daughter Mary Elizabeth, a registered nurse, would be in a hospital caring for the sick and injured. My son William, an aspiring linguist, might be called on to perform translating services for Hispanic families in need of help. My son John, a social worker, would be needed to place children in foster care services. My daughter Rachel, a teacher, might be asked to work with displaced school children to keep them up to date with their course work. And my son Thomas, a journalist, would be needed to write the personal stories and events of those that had been affected by the disaster. The presence of diversity in this one family alone might mean the difference between life and death for those who receive their services!

Obviously, they did not all learn in the same way. They all had different interests and perspectives. One factor that Elizabeth and I have emphatically stressed to all our children is that the relative worth of each person's work is unknowable. All contribute to the entire culture. The plumber and the dishwasher are just as necessary as the teacher, the scientist, and the owner of a business. In a culturally responsive aspect of milieu, there is individual capacity and responsibility, but not individualism. Social and political awareness are always in the making, as individual capacities, strengths, and perspectives are not just tolerated, but welcomed.

The language of imaginative milieu is characterized by fluidity and flexibility that resists predefinition, dead metaphor, and second hand meaning in every domain of knowledge. Instead, the prevailing language is created out of personal connection through metaphoric and experiential blending of the old and the newly conceived. In this milieu, the process of personal meaning formation is just as important as the product. This is an area where milieu overlaps with subject matter. Nevertheless, this element of milieu is one of the most important discoveries I have made in this inquiry! Indeed, writing as a form of inquiry has proven to be the vehicle and one of the most important destinations in the process of writing this book.

The act of thinking as writing has enabled me to articulate some deeply held thoughts that I have pondered for many years. The ideas I encountered in all of my reading for the last ten years and a lifetime of personal experiences came together through this process. But this required the kind of critical pondering of given concepts, traditional thinking, and clichés that brings to mind the metaphor of cleaning out your closet and throwing away worn out clothes, or turning them into cleaning rags because if they were too far gone for your own personal use, why give them to anyone else? Dewey said the "conscious adjustment between the new and old is imagination" (1934, p. 272). This milieu welcomes that adjustment, and writing helps us to distinguish between the new and old, so that we can either throw out the old or conjoin it with the new.

This milieu operates on organic time, not mass production time. Personal meaning and discovery necessitates a milieu of incubation. In this inquiry I have learned that this is one of the greatest features of a curriculum of imagination. Sensed gaps, found problems, and personal questions have the power to implore the learner into the environment of incubation, where the learner has space to creatively and critically think things through. Teachers and parents need to carefully respect the organic and personal processes that are required for each one to peck their own way out of the shell. This can take many forms. I have already mentioned that I have had many fruitful episodes of rumination while mowing the lawn or riding a bicycle, as well as times that were so quiet that I was aware of my heart pumping blood all the way to my feet. Of course, this is not always possible in school, but I feel very strongly about making room for silent reading and writing and some form of incubation "time." There are times when learners like Qui Liang that I mentioned in a previous chapter need time to adjust inwardly to a new culture and time to be allowed to make metaphoric connections.

Also, there is little doubt that Einstein's notion of the relativity of time and motion was brought to articulation after a long period of incubation. It also seems plausible that Rosa Parks passed through an incubation period after the seeds of change were sown in her by contact with others who sensed large gaps of injustice. Out of an incubation period, there emerged a critical moment of action that released a whole chain of events. This aspect of milieu is tragically lacking in an age of instant information, drive-through dining, and performance standards that specify exactly what content should be covered and how long that should take.

Freire's notion of critical consciousness is also an aspect of milieu, but again there is an overlap with subject matter and teacher. Critical consciousness should be thought of as more of a continually active process of thought, so I will position it as part of the milieu "that links the creation of critical citizens to the development of a radical democracy" (Aronowitz & Giroux, 1991, p. 188). This focus hearkens back to one of my original questions about how imagination can help create political awareness. As I thought of ways that Freire might apply critical consciousness for the 21st century, I decided to do a simple internet search and see what it might yield. I found a website for the Center for Media Literacy and was surprised to find that its theoretical framework is based on Freire's concept of critical literacy and problem-posing education. Through the influence of Freire's writing, the founder, Elizabeth Thoman, came up with this underlying methodology:

> Through a four-step "inquiry" process of Awareness, Analysis, Reflection, and Action, media literacy helps young people acquire an empowering set of "navigational" skills which include the ability to: Access information from a variety of sources, analyze and explore how messages are "constructed"

whether print, verbal, visual or multi-media, evaluate media's explicit and implicit messages against one's own ethical, moral and/or democratic principles. Express or create their own messages using a variety of media tools. (Center for Media Literacy, 2002, n.p.)

One of the best samples of the work of this group is the presentation of *Five Key Questions That Can Change the World* (Share, Jolls, & Thoman, 2005). These questions, in one form or another, are consistent with my understanding of a curriculum of imagination in the making. They are as follows:

Who created this message? What creative techniques are used to attract my attention? How might different people understand this message differently than me? What values, lifestyles, and points of view are represented in, or omitted from, this message? Why is this message being sent? (p. 9)

These same questions are broken down for young children like this:

What is this? How is it put together? What do I see or hear, smell, touch or taste? What do I like or dislike about this? What might other people think and feel about this? What do I think and feel about this? What does this tell me about how other people live and behave? Is anything or anyone left out? Is this trying to tell me something? Is this trying to sell me something? (p. 12)

This simplified version still asks potent questions and provides a foundation for getting children to think about these kinds of issues even in elementary schools. We certainly know that advertisers understand the power of their influence with young children. Teachers should use their personal influence to counteract this by cultivating a culture of critical and personal questioning each student. Certainly this is part of what it means to use the imagination to sense gaps. It is out of the sense that something is missing that creativity, through the world-making power of imagination, brings forth changes in every domain, both public and private. Through the impartation of critical consciousness, the act of creating or recreating can begin in childhood and extend through a whole lifetime.

The milieu of a curriculum of imagination should inspire people more to inquire, rather than provide answers in isolated and decontextualized ways to questions that students are not asking. When I look at all these features together as part of a commonplace of a curriculum of imagination, the milieu is one of hope and possibility that encourages growth beyond the confines of controlled meaning and orthodox interpretation. This milieu cultivates personal incubation in organic time instead of the "mass production" concept of standardization. In addition, the milieu of a curriculum of imagination maintains a continual consciousness that critically questions relationships of power, influence, and static meaning. But before moving on to the next commonplace, the social and communal aspects of milieu, as well as the sense of belonging and care, need to be addressed.

Dialogue across differences is another key element in imaginative milieu. This should be welcomed in every role of relationship. Parents, policymakers, teachers, learners, community members, and all stakeholders in education need to be brought under the influence of the power of dialogue and the auditory aspect of curriculum as conversation. As I noted in Chapter 5, the ability to listen requires imagination because, by its influence, we are able to hear multiple meanings presented in polyphonic sounds that require inner attunement, not just the narrow sounds of cliché or the kind of inward thoughts that cause knee-jerk reactions to what we hear. The prejudiced person is only in tune with himself or herself. Through this inquiry, I have been made more aware that this is one of the greatest needs in the culture of education and certainly should be included in any form of imaginative milieu.

The last element that I discovered really includes all the others. It is the sense of belonging and personal care that is present when all the other aspects of imaginative milieu are contributing to the environment. When every voice is welcomed and personal meaning is treasured, when organic time to incubate is honored and the art of imaginative listening is continually cultivated and difference is seen as strength, not weakness, the sense of belonging and personal care will certainly flourish. In this milieu, critical consciousness and questioning will become more effective because learners will be less likely to be cynical in an environment of hope. By the same token, hope can become more substantial when myth and cliché, stereotype and insincerity are brought to the light by critical questioning.

Imaginative Teacher

My understanding of the commonplace of the teacher in a curriculum of imagination has been shaped very strongly by Freire's concept of critical pedagogy. In this perspective, the teacher is also a learner. In the milieu of dialogue, the teacher and the learner discover together. I am privileged to have been a student at Empire State College for my undergraduate work. This program allows you to design your own coursework within the parameters of the degree you pursue. In fact, one of the courses we received credit for was based on how well we designed our own curriculum. For one of my senior electives, I created a course on the history and performance of American Folk Music. When I defended my written paper and literally performed the content with a guitar, my teacher, who was a very well trained violinist, commented on what she had learned from the experience. She also asked spontaneous questions out of her genuine interest, throughout the assessment event.

This is a perfect example of the kind of organic overlapping that occurs between the commonplaces in a curriculum of imagination. As the learner, I was encouraged to follow my own interests in designing a course. I was placed with a teacher who possessed highly refined abilities in the field of classical music, and yet, through her questions, she brought things to my attention about my own playing that I had never articulated before. She specifically commented on what she had learned. Another teacher I had in the same program would ask me what I wanted to learn. We would actually negotiate the content of our course together. He would end the negotiation by saying, "That sounds good, Bob; I look forward to learning from you." I would then be sent on my way to read and write papers and return in a few weeks to dialogue about what I had learned. Of course, this was also a time of defense as the teacher critically questioned the logic, form, and content of my writing. All of this was done out of a posture of equality and personal care that created the space for confrontation without falling into the trap of taking his criticism personally. I broke out of a rut in my thinking and writing while I worked with this teacher. He told me not to be so stingy with words. He said that I should always write in a personal way and not apologize for it. I was encouraged to let go of the passive voice and actively express my feelings and preferences. This was entirely new to me, and it is an ongoing endeavor. In fact, the process of spontaneous release and freely sharing my perspectives in writing has been constantly drawn out of me by Ming Fang He and William Schubert throughout this inquiry. Through their words and examples, I realize with new clarity, as with every other form of artistic expression, writing is serious work that requires constant creation, reflection, and recreation.

Looking back on these experiences, through the lens of this present inquiry, I have come to understand the teacher as an improvisational artist (Bateson, 1989) who has the flexibility to work spontaneously and yet deliberately toward the opening of creative vision and expression in learners. This notion reminds be of something that my wife Elizabeth's art teacher told her when she began oil painting classes. "I can't teach you to paint, but I can teach you to see" (personal communication, 2003). That statement says so much about the teacher as an improvisational artist. In this role, the teacher helps to give birth to personalized meaning and self-expression and, at the same time, challenges the learner to greater quality through appropriate criticism. Individual care and concern and an awareness of the process of organic time in the learner is of primary concern. By this, I am not referring to generalized categories of lifespan developmental psychology. This knowledge is more intuitive than information derived from a collection of pathologies that are applied in an objective way. What I have come to understand instead is that a curriculum of imagination is a relationship between the teacher and the learner wherein both teacher and learner exercise reflective, critical, and generative imagination to discover, express, and evaluate desired learning.

The conjoining of creative and critical aspects brings me to another dimension of the teacher in a curriculum of imagination that should be included. This is the notion of the teacher as a connoisseur (Eisner, 1998a); this role is important "in any realm in which the character, import, or value of objects, situations, and performances is distributed and variable, including educational practice" (p. 63). The critic is the public side of the same role. "Connoisseurs simply need to appreciate what they encounter. Critics, however, must render these qualities vivid, by the artful use of critical disclosure" (Eisner, 1985, pp. 92–93). By presenting connoisseurship and criticism as two aspects of the same concept, Eisner supports a creative/critical aspect of imagination that helps to recognize and distinguish the finely nuanced aspects in every domain of inquiry. The critical aspect is the public expression of connoisseurship that involves the communication of detailed distinctions in such a way that they are recognized and understood by others.

I remember being awakened to the genius of one of the greatest bass guitar players of all time, through both verbal and musical expression, by the members of a band I was in as a teenager. One of the band members said, "Listen man; that's James Jamerson!" After being taught to listen and notice what I might not have been aware of otherwise, I am always eager to share what I have learned. Now, I tell my children to listen for nuances in the bass line all the time. This same notion of connoisseurship and criticism could be used to cause others to notice anything, from the practical uses of the Pythagorean theory, to the power of propaganda, to the perspective of sunlight in fine art. The connoisseur/critic is certainly an essential feature of the teacher in a curriculum of imagination!

A teacher should be a living sample of what is taught. If the teacher expects the learner be a passionate inquirer, he or she must also express the demeanor of always being onto something new, never static or dogmatic, but open and aware that growth is the only sign of life. This inward vitality will come through even when the teacher performs the "traditional" roles of classroom discussion on the forms that comprise the foundation for further inquiry. This could be anything from punctuation to the best way to prepare pie crusts.

By using the deductive aspect of writing in this instance, I conclude that in a curriculum of imagination in the making, the teacher is a learner, improvisational artist, and a model of what is taught. As a learner, he or she discovers meaning in a shared ontology. Education is dialogue, and conversation and the participants all have something added to their understanding. As an improvisational artist, the teacher helps create personalized meaning and self-expression in the learner through personal concern and care along with intuitive sense of timing and understanding of the learner potential. This requires both the creative and critical aspects of imagination in every encounter with the student. You cannot give what you do not have yourself. A teacher of curriculum of imagination must be a living model by refusing static meaning and dead metaphors and by actively engaging in a passionate pursuit of understanding, while at the same time being willing to admit that he or she is still learning. This is what this inquiry has taught me about the commonplace of the teacher.

Imaginative Subject Matter

In this inquiry, I first discovered what the commonplace of the subject matter in a curriculum of imagination is by contrasting it with standardized and static knowledge. I saw, for example, the lack of engagement that is present when the subject matter is presented in isolated and decontextualized units as a product of the canon of "official knowledge" (Apple, 1993). This is often enforced on passive recipients who have learned to play the game in order to get a good grade, or by the same token, to those who despair because their real strengths are not measured by tests of standardized subject matter. This condition has been further exacerbated by "accountability" requirements from both federal and state legislation in the form of "benchmarks" in the No Child Left Behind Act of 2003 (U.S. Department of Education, 2005) and the new Georgia Quality Core Curriculum (Georgia Department of Education, 2005) and similar practices in other states. This curriculum is mostly prescriptive and confining rather than descriptive and narrative of actual lived experience.

Also, the subject matter of a standardized curriculum is comprised of objective facts and skills that are often detached from real-life contexts by rote and mechanistic imitation. Often this is accomplished through means of verbal learning alone. I love how Lisa Delpit (1995) described the way this approach might be used to teach African Americans to dance. This would involve a workbook with "200 hundred mastery units" for each dance (p. 39) and, as a result, at the end of the year, there would be many

African American students in remedial dance classes No! We learn to dance by dancing.

In a curriculum of imagination in the making, the commonplace of the subject matter is boundless and multidimensional, yet holistic and personal. It is not contained in any one discipline but shuns fragmentation. It welcomes multiple meanings and newly created metaphoric connections. The only limitations on its scope are the present circumscribed horizons of the imaginer. The subject matter can be anything from the microcosm or subatomic dimension to the macrocosm, so many light years away that even the most powerful telescope on earth cannot detect its presence because any light that may be present is still so distant that it is out of the range of measurement.

I have discovered that in the actual experience of the dynamic of a curriculum of imagination, the dichotomy between objective and subjective understanding disappears. This happens when the subject matter is acquired through a metaphoric blending of the old with the new, lived experience with the inexperienced, and the emotions along with mental faculties. It is through these connections that subject matter becomes personal as well as social. This takes place through the language of metaphor, a very important component of the commonplace of subject matter in a curriculum of imagination. In fact, I have learned that it is almost impossible to exercise imagination about any subject matter without metaphor. This was easy for me to understand in grasping personal meaning because metaphor is simply seeing one new concept through one that is already part of one's personal schema. One completely new part of this for me was the use of metaphor when the subject matter is the "other." How thrilled I was to read Ozick (1991) on this matter! She says, "Metaphor is the reciprocal agent, the universalizing force: it makes possible the power to envision the stranger's heart" (p. 279). By metaphor, we are able to see our lives in the lives of others. This has very important social and political implications for reaching out across barriers in so much more than a superficial, patronizing way. Metaphor has the power to create empathy by revealing human connections that transcend race, class, gender, and ethnicity.

The subject matter of imagination welcomes polyphonic expression and dialogue across differences because the exact same subject matter could have a range of meanings to individual learners. The focus of learning can be on anything that the imaginer can question or wonder about. In fact, the subject matter often makes itself known through questions that arise out of sensed gaps from within or found problems. The subject matter is multidimensional because in the realm of imagination, objective notions become personalized through metaphoric blending and repeated musings until new connections are made and new applications are discovered.

I have also learned that subject matter of this kind is holistically explored across multiple content areas. For example, my son William wrote a paper for a math class several years ago about the use of algebraic computation in the computer programming language that is needed to create video games. He also is learning music composition through the soundtrack of video games. In the subject matter of a curriculum of imagination, the whole universe and all that is in it can be a text.

Imaginative Learner

This inquiry into a curriculum of imagination came out of my own desire to understand who I am as a learner, in a way that would help me understand all learners. In the process, I began to see the learner in three dimensions: the learner as inquirer, intern, and creator. As I recall my own personal history of discovery, I recognize points in my life when imagination is conspicuous by its absence, as well as its presence. This contrast is what initiated the formal stage of this inquiry over two years ago, when I first articulated a general form of the questions I have sought to answer through this work.

The principle of contrast is intensified by what appeared to be a sociocultural trend toward increased standardization on a variety of fronts, and in particular, in the field of education. In this context, the features of an imaginative learner were made salient. The imaginative learner has a spirit of exploration and Freire's notion of "critical consciousness" simultaneously by embracing the unknown and imagining against the grain. When faced with contradiction and obstacles of every kind, the imaginative learner refuses stasis and the line of least resistance and challenges orthodox thinking.

My understanding of the role of imagination in the learner as inquirer did not start with school experience. As I have already mentioned, my progress in formal education as a child and adolescent was far from being illustrious. Almost all of the breakthroughs of discovery or accomplishment I can recall occurred outside of the classroom. Music has played such an important role in my journey as a learner, and yet one of the D's I received in kindergarten was in music class.

In the prologue, I mentioned how I began my career in music by playing spoons on jars of water. Of course, I was not aware of all that I was learning about sound waves and scales, nor was I aware of the foundation that this form of play as inquiry was giving me for other aspects of imagination. In retrospect, I understand the immense significance of inquiry that is initiated within the student and was confirmed by all that I learned from Dewey's writing. This can be summed up by saying that the learner is not made for the curriculum; a curriculum of imagination in the making begins through the inquiry of the learner.

I can see now that the experience with the canning jars helped me to teach myself how to play the blues harmonica. There is so much about this genre of music that is intuitive. I remember reading a few sentences of "method" on the paper insert enclosed in my newly purchased instrument, but learning to play was a matter of personal and passionate inquiry of the imagination, first of all through *reflecting* the sounds I heard being played by others, and then *generating* my own signature sounds. This experience led me directly to the intern dimension of learning. I had already taught myself the basics of the guitar, so when I was asked to join a band and play the harmonica, I became a guitar intern as well. I learned quite a bit by observation, as well as direct instruction from the lead guitar player. Out of that experience, I came to understand imagination in its creative or generative aspect by creating my own emphasis or personal slant of a combination of technique and the very personal domain of the emotions. It was only in the last year, as I sought a formal definition of imagination, that I was able to name these early experiences in these terms. But having done so, I am able to recognize their features in all learners in one degree or another.

One of my favorite books as a child was the biography of the Wright Brothers written by Quentin Reynolds (1950). It is easy to recognize the role that passionate inquiry played in their identity as learners. Out of their own desire to know, they diligently read and applied all the previous body of knowledge about flight and all else that could be known about the principles of aerodynamics. I now understand this as a curriculum of reflective imagination in the making. Here, the two brothers are marked as interns to the given body of knowledge and to each other as they experimented with flight. These experiences brought them to the dimension of learners as creators, and through many painful episodes of sensing gaps, problem finding, and creative and critical thinking, they changed the culture of the entire world.

This reflection on my own experience and the experience of learners in every sphere of discovery, along with the theoretical understanding I have gained through this inquiry, brings me to this conclusion about the commonplace of the learner in a curriculum of imagination: The learner is first an inquirer, seeking personal understanding out of his or her own desires, interests, aptitudes, and questions. This is likely to bring the learner into an internship with given forms of knowledge and experiences with others, either directly or indirectly. Through sensing gaps in the predefined body of knowledge and questioning the status quo in every given domain, the learner enters into the dimension of generative imagination as a creator.

Curriculum of Imagination in the Making

Through these four commonplaces, I recognize a living configuration of imaginative curriculum that is both theoretical and practical. At the same time, I acknowledge that a curriculum of imagination can never be turned into a method of the recipe variety. It is not an a priori form to be mass produced with singular specifications; it is constantly created through engaging and participatory discovery. There are aspects that are learned with others, of course, but just as every human is unique, life itself is never static in its creative dynamic. No two trees are exactly alike, but when they stop growing, they are dead. And yet every living thing is dependent on others within the same species in order to perpetuate life. Even a stalk of corn must interact with others in order to produce nutrition; otherwise, it is just a weed. Imagination expresses these features of the power of life in vibrant and creative milieus, teachers, learners, and subject matter.

The sphere of life is never static; it is constantly changing and being changed by the environment of social, political, and natural movement, through forces of self-preservation. Education is a very important aspect of the sphere of life, in which the power of biological, sociological, and cultural sustainability is either directly or indirectly passed on to succeeding generations. Education needs to continually renew itself through continual creative reflection and action, and a curriculum of imagination is always in the making. In the examples I have used throughout this inquiry, this is an emerging theme, although I never fully noticed it until I was writing this section.

As I look back over what I have written, I recognize an element that unites all of the four commonplaces in holistic critical mass. It is the principle of life itself, active and dynamically present within each commonplace that creates a condition out of which personal meaning is continually created *from within* the participants. After returning to the opening conversation between Greene and Freire about old worldviews of imagination, metaphor, and "pure rational thought," I see newly created connections between those ideas in both democracy and curriculum in the making.

Imagination is so much more than the recreation of Plato's notion of ideal forms that take the focus off the present and into the past. A curriculum of imagination exists in the present tense as it responds to what *is*, not what *was*. Metaphor goes far beyond the rhetorical use of comparing two similar items. Metaphor combines schemata with present experience and creates new ways of seeing, knowing, experiencing, and communicating in the sphere of life.

The highest kind of thinking is not void of emotion or the engagement of the physical senses. It involves the whole being through imaginative connections, in naming and transforming from within. These are a few of the notions from the early part of this book that stand out in bold relief for me, as I view democracy in the making, as a metaphor for a curriculum of imagination in the making. For example, the problem with an externalized configuration of "democracy" that did not arise from an inward passion of the people but that came about through a surface level assent to a new government is that it results in what Freire called adaptation. The metaphor of the banking model of education can also apply to political change on a national scale as well.

> It is not surprising that the banking concept of education regards men as adaptable, manageable beings. The more students work at storing the deposits entrusted to them, the less they develop the critical consciousness which would result from their intervention in the world as transformers of that world. The more completely they accept the passive role imposed on them, the more they tend simply to adapt to the world as it is and to the fragmented view of reality deposited in them. (Freire, 1970, p. 73)

When America revolted against England, transformation came from an awakened citizenry that named their walls and put their own lives on the line to move beyond the control of the political and religious empire of colonialism. At present, special interest groups deafen the voices of democratic conversation. The ensuing crisis over the tolerance of this condition is keenly felt in our schools. Neither education nor democracy is a product that can be governed like a corporation. As Dewey said, "Democracy must be born anew in every generation, and education is its midwife" (1916, p. 139). There can be no finalized and completed form of democracy or a curriculum of imagination. This is why sensing gaps, raising questions, and challenging the given and the static are such important concepts. In the environment of ongoing inquiry, constant innovation and critical appraisal, there is life, and where there is life, there is a curriculum of imagination in the making, connecting the known with the newly discovered.

A curriculum of imagination is not a pattern to be recreated. Of course the nature of education requires that deliberate plans be made and content covered. But the planned curriculum never trumps the enacted curriculum when imagination is at work, because the focused objectives in a curriculum of imagination are not external benchmarks to be attained. Instead they are embodied texts that are made alive through creative presentation and internalized through the personal construction of meaning. In a curriculum of imagination, the focus in always on the process, on becoming the continuously rewritten text and not a finished product, as Dewey so eloquently put it over 100 years ago. "Thinking is not like a sausage machine which reduces all materials indifferently to one marketable commodity, but is a power of following up and linking" (1910/1933, p. 39).

In a curriculum of imagination, critical and creative thinking are never treated as separate and distinct operations. Imagination is needed in sensing gaps, naming walls, challenging mediocrity, and uncovering deception or in deconstructing obsolete and static forms of thinking. But at the same time, imagination implores us to inquire, create, and discover afresh as Freire (1998) observes imaginative learners:

> The Learners maintain alive the flame of resistance that sharpens their curiosity and stimulates their capacity for risk, for adventure so as to immunize themselves against the banking system [of education]. In this sense, the creative force of the learning process, which encompasses comparison, repetition, observation, indomitable doubt, and curiosity not easily satisfied, overcomes the negative effects of the false teaching. (Freire, 1998, p. 32)

The field of education is replete with valid critique through the deconstruction of discourses that are unjust and hegemonic. But without an emphasis on "epistemological curiosity" (Freire, 1998) the spirit of inquiry turns sour very quickly. A curriculum of imagination is a curriculum of hope because it enables the "naming of walls" (Greene, 1988), but also creates a language for freedom and possibility (Rasheed, 2007).

A curriculum of imagination is not just designated to the confines of school, but embraces the entire life of the learner. Schubert (2009) comments astutely on Dewey's vision of Utopia where there are "no schools at all. Education is carried on without anything of the nature of schools" (p. 19). Later in the chapter, Schubert comments on out of school learning experiences:

> [N]o one should certify on matters of one's personal growth, except the inner being of those who have the experience. Really who dares to *certify?* Who really knows what is embodied in another, derived from any experience—school or non-school? Yet, the big question is: Who benefits from certification? Is it not those who are positions to acquire most from the sorting machine? (p. 23)

In a curriculum of imagination there is no need for a "sorting machine" that places students who have a hard time sitting passively still, whose minds are unstandardizable into "alternative schools" or the "vocational track" often as a punitive measure. In a curriculum of imagination, the lines between hands-on learning and academic subjects are strongly blurred or nonexistent so much that there is no stigma attached to vocational or technical training.

In a curriculum of imagination, every voice is invited "into the art of this conversation in which we learn to recognize the voices, each conditioned by a different perception of the world" (H. L. Gates, quoted in Greene, 1995, p. 156). Imaginative listening that is able to resonate empathically with those who are "other" no matter what the designation of "other" might be creates the capacity for imaginative communication that does not respond out of habitual reaction through prejudgments, stereotypes, and scripted responses.

These areas are just a very few broad strokes of rendering a curriculum of imagination. There is no "snapshot" available and no conclusion possible. Instead of sensing a finished product that I can close the door upon, I now see many more doors that are opened before me. The conversation is gloriously incomplete! I am reminded of T. S. Eliot's lines from *Four Quartets*.

> We shall not cease from exploration
> And the end of all our exploring
> Will be to arrive where we started
> And know the place for the first time. (1943, p. 59)

Epilogue

"He not busy being born is busy dying."
—Bob Dylan (1965)

"Keep asking, and keep wondering. It will keep you alive."
—Maxine Greene (2001, p. 91)

This epilogue now comes at the end of over ten years of work in writing, and yet my level of curiosity and passion for understanding a curriculum of imagination has steadily increased though this entire endeavor. As I have said several times throughout this work, a curriculum of imagination is always in the making, and I expect to be recreating my understanding in this domain for the rest of my life.

Now more than ever, I am aware of walls of standardization and the infiltration of the business model into places of learning at every level. Yet at the same time, I have an even greater sense of hope and a desire to release imagination in response to these tensions through a steady yet broad flow of the range of ideas. I will discuss a few of them here.

The area of tension that comes immediately to mind has to do with imagination in academic writing and is summed up in this question: How can we explore new forms of imaginative writing while maintaining integrity and truthfulness about our subject(s)?

A Curriculum of Imagination in an Era of Standardization, pages 107–113
Copyright © 2013 by Information Age Publishing
All rights of reproduction in any form reserved.

Eisner (2005) expresses this tension well:

> One of the most significant shifts occurring in the educational research community is the broadening of its conception of what counts as educational research. This increased breadth is not a license for anything goes but a recognition that the roads to understanding are many and a narrow view of method is likely to lead to limited understanding of how. (p. 161)

A primary example, of course is the "imaginary dialogue" in this book. This is an area where peer review and validity comparisons as well as careful readings of related literature in context are so important. Another example comes from my work with graduate students by using other genres and discourses of writing and representation of research that break with the norm, while thoroughly fulfilling scholarly expectations and purposes. Another area would involve the use of drama and the arts to accompany the written texts. There are many others working in the domain already, but there is plenty more to be discovered and expressed in this area.

At present I am extending this area of interest in epistolary inquiry by editing and contributing to three books of letters. These three volumes express imaginative writing in a number of ways including the use of poetry, dance, scriptwriting, graphic novel formats, in capturing unique reflections on the lives and scholarship of Maxine Greene (Lake, 2010) and Nel Noddings (Lake, 2012). These books have presented a way to acknowledge and in some cases expand on the scholarship of those to whom they are addressed without the limitation of the standard festschrift form. Also, the letter format adds a humanizing quality to the style of writing that is often missing in academic prose.

The third book that I co-edited with Tricia Kress (2012) is called: *We Saved the Best for You: Letters of Hope, Imagination and Wisdom to 21st Century Educators.* My hope is that the contributors will render a composite vision that implores the present and future generation of educators to see beyond the nightmarish present of dehumanization, bullying, violence, the disease of cynicism, and increasing "*stasis* and the *flatness* of ordinary life" (Greene, 1988, p. 123) that is the result of the standardization of "official knowledge" (Apple, 1993) and what the artist/scientist Bob Miller calls "hardening of the categories" (in Lake, 2010, p. 15). We have subconsciously or conscientiously sent a message to the young that the collective culture of the past was "better" and you "should have been there." We owe this vision of what can be to our students, children, grandchildren, and great grandchildren, and imagination is at its best in the articulation of the possible.

Another of the foremost questions emerging from this inquiry is: How can metaphor as the language of the imagination become more conspicuous in the field of education, and what are some of the ways to apply it to every level of learning, including early literacy experiences? It should come as no surprise to know that children are great at creating their own metaphors. Winner and Gardner (1993) found that children "performed as well as adults when asked to explain the similarity underlying the perceptual metaphors" (p. 432). In every level of education, and across all content areas, metaphor as the language of imagination should be increasingly cultivated by means of movement, sound, art, conversation, and pictorial representation through technology and literature.

Another crucial question that arises from this writing experience is: How can writing as learning be more fully implemented in every level and domain of education?

The whole experience of writing this inquiry has served to heighten my interest in Laurel Richardson's work in writing as "a method of inquiry" (2003). This has implications for every grade level. I would like to apply this notion to K–12 education in connection with portfolio creation and writing across content areas. Writing as thinking and reading is already being used in so many ways, but I would also seek to adapt this method to early literacy experiences in conjunction with metaphor creation in children. I also want to explore ways that this notion can be applied to the learning experiences of vocational education students in a way that starts with engagement of hands-on content areas and ends with narrative writing. The cart has been put before the horse in this area for too long! Many of these students are never allowed to pursue their interests because they have to jump through so many standardized testing hoops before they can actually engage their interests. This often results in further marginalization by limited employment options and the resulting negative social effects.

It is only recently that I have come to recognize the immense value of Louise Rosenblatt's work in connection with the content of this inquiry. And out of that has come a desire to help my students recognize ways that imaginative connections, in which objective and subjective distinctions are removed, can be used in a constructivist approach to reading, even at the elementary school level. Rosenblatt has a place with both Greene and Freire's notions of plurality of meaning in the text and the praxis of emancipatory literacy. Here she introduces this continuum of efferent vs. aesthetic reading:

> To abstract the information or the directions for action needed after reading a sociological essay or a medical report, for example, the reader must focus attention primarily on the impersonal, publicly verifiable aspects of what the words evoke and must be subordinate or push into the fringes of consciousness the affective aspects. I term this efferent reading, from the

Latin *efferre* "to carry away." To produce a poem or play, the reader must broaden the scope of attention to include the personal, affective aura and associations surrounding the words evoked and must focus on—experience, live through—the moods, scenes, situations being created during the transaction. I term this "*aesthetic*" reading. These stances are not opposites but form a continuum of possible transactions with a text. According to different purposes, readings of the same text may fall at different points on the efferent–aesthetic continuum, on different 'mixes' of attention to public and private aspects. Much of our reading falls in the middle of the continuum, hence the need to adopt an appropriate selective stance. Traditional teaching—and testing—methods often confuse the student by implicitly fostering a nonliterary, efferent approach when the actual purpose is presumably an aesthetic reading. (Rosenblatt, 1995, p. xvii)

I hope to deepen my understanding of ways to connect this theory with the content of this inquiry, through both teaching and writing, in ways that would move content area subjects closer to the aesthetic side of the continuum. Egan (1997) discusses ways that content can be placed into story form in ways that engage the material through the emotions. What possibilities there are here!

If you think of the lesson or unit more like telling a good story than conveying a body of information, then the need to focus on how to tell the story as crisply as possible comes to the fore rather than the attempt to meet sets of knowledge, skills, and attitude objectives. If the story is told well, such objectives will be met in a more meaningful context. (p. 248)

This inquiry has stirred my interest in personal story and dialogue across differences, as a key to moving beyond superficial multiculturalism. As a teacher educator I am confronted with the tension of challenging students toward diversity in a rural setting where, all too often, stereotypical thinking runs rampant. One of the ways I have been able to challenge these attitudes is to have the students start with telling their own stories in a way that affirms their sense of place and then, through interview assignments and class readings and working in small groups together, the students are able to find surprising places of empathy and openness. This is vitally important for anyone and especially for future teachers. I agree with Maxine Greene on this when she presents the tension in this manner: "If we break through and even disrupt a surface equilibrium and uniformity, this does not mean that particular ethnic or racial traditions ought to replace our own" (Greene, 1993, p. 15). In the same article, Greene goes on to quote from Freire and Macedo:

Every person ought, on some level cherish her or his culture; but it should never be absolutized. When it is absolutized and a person is closed against the new culture and surrounding him or her, you would even find it hard to learn new things which placed alongside your personal history can be meaningful. (p. 16)

This space of tension between cultivating my students' sense of place and acknowledging the dangers of "absolutized" cultural sense of self has provided a dialectical approach to learning that mostly all of the students have benefitted from to one degree or another. Here are a few excerpts from my class assignments that I am using with the permission of the students:

I have to admit that now that I am at the completion of this class, I now have a more open mind to others around me. I noticed that just because the girl sitting next to me is the same race as me doesn't mean she feels the same way on certain topics. For instance one day our class was discussing our relationships with our parents. The girl next to me seemed to be a mama's girl that likes to be the girly girl. It turned out that she plays rugby and talks to her dad on a daily basis. (Stephanie Mincey, 2010)

Another student comments on the story of a classmate who up until recently was an "unregistered alien." She is in fact, one of my best students last year and her story touched each of us profoundly.

What I view as the turning point was when a female student in class opened up about the Mexican *coyotes*. I had never heard this term before, and in all honesty I just assumed that people who crossed the border merely had to walk across a fence when a guard's back was turned and they were in. It was seeing the raw human struggle that changed me. All of a sudden, the term *illegal alien* was no longer some abstract concept attached to a subhuman, taco eating fiend, it was someone's mother. It was a she, and that started a change in me. (Nico Adams, 2010)

Finally, I share this narrative from a teacher who was empowered to act.

I recently...was asked by the principal to sit in as a member on retention meetings for 8th grade students who did not pass the dreaded CRCT [Criterion-Referenced Competency Test]. At first I was apprehensive because I thought to myself, "I do not want to hear the same old stories again." My line of thinking then changed. I remembered what I read in the book about speaking out for injustices so I accepted the invitation. At the meetings, I spoke out for those children whose lives were being affected by a committee of people (six to be exact) who did not really know them or their situations. I spoke out for those children using the words, the content, and the knowledge I've acquired from the readings and resources in this class.

The committee members looked at me as if they were seeing me for the first time. I truly became an advocate for those students and I did not quiet down. Dr. Lake, they were ALL children of color and/or poverty. (Kathy Flowers, 2010)

In the context of the current "English only" debate and immigration reform, I would also like build upon the notion of multiple ways of knowing, seeing, metaphor formation, language ego, and discourse by seeking connections of this inquiry to the dual immersion model of bilingual education as described by Johnson and Swain (1997):

> Given the core features we have proposed, we would argue that there are some programs labeled immersion that have overextended the use of this term to the point at which a discussion of common issues and problems becomes difficult, if not impossible. A good example of inappropriate over-extension is the labeling of English-only programs for Spanish-speaking minorities in the United States as "immersion education." Such English-only education leads to replacive or subtractive bilingualism in the academic domain, while the wide use of the L2 in public domains leads to the development of interpersonal and social proficiency that immersion students do not have the opportunity to acquire. (p. 12)

My guiding questions in continuing this study would focus on whether or not bilingual fluency has any bearing on increasing creativity and personal agency in both personal and social aspects of problem finding and problem solving. I also would like to inquire further about cross-cultural and decolonializing identity formation found in the work of Mohanty (2003), He (2003), Igoa (1995), and others.

I am still fascinated with the notion of incubation and how it might be used in all content areas and both personal and social breakthroughs. I would like to study the lives of teachers, parents, social activists, artists, inventors, philosophers, farmers, writers, engineers, mathematicians, carpenters, musicians, and more to discover the role of incubation in the creative process.

I will continue to explore ways to use music and multiple literacies across content areas. Recent studies suggest that there is a connection between playing music and divergent/creative thinking (Vanderbilt University, 2008). I would like to design courses for several different age groups that combined the history of philosophy along with the history of music and art. I feel like I have only scratched the surface in understanding how all of the various modes of seeing, hearing, thinking, feeling, and moving can be used to fully engage and enhance other forms of literacy. Since the culture of education is still so strongly dominated by verbal literacy and written communication skills serve as a gatekeeper to so many more opportunities, I would like to spend at least 20 more years exploring ways to connect each learner's inner landscape with the ability to think creatively and critically and communicate in every discourse available to humans.

While working on this book, I took many breaks from writing and reading by walking in the woods behind our house. The path I chose would take almost an hour to complete, so it provided me with a lot of "incubation" time as well as exercise. At my halfway point is a small pond with an area for fishing. Next to the pond is a fish-cleaning table that was made from an old millstone for grinding wheat or corn in the way that my ancestors did. I always touch that stone and feel the ridges in it, as if by that act, I could reach back across time even 50 years to the lives of my forbears, in their lived worlds, as sharecroppers on my mother's side, and migrant loggers in the great North woods on my father's side.

On the third turn in my walk, I stop to listen to a small stream as it flows through a cypress swamp and watch as a lovely white heron often stops to drink there. In the sound of running water, I hear the ever flowing voice of imagination, and by its gentle singing, I am aware that by its peaceful and persistent influence, I imagine myself as part of a bridge between one generation of sharecroppers and migrant loggers to all that my own children and grandchildren and students are becoming, and I am compelled and inspired to press on.

References

Akeroyd, R. (1986). *The word* [Cassette]. Louisville, KY: Beadle.

Apple, M. (1993). *Official knowledge: Democratic education in a conservative age.* New York, NY: Rutledge.

Apple, M. (2001). *Educating the "right" way: Markets, standards, God and inequality.* New York, NY: Routledge Falmer.

Applebee, A. N. (1996). *Curriculum as conversation: Transforming traditions of teaching and learning.* Chicago, IL: University of Chicago Press.

Aristotle. (n.d.). *Rhetoric.* (W. Rhys Roberts, Trans.). Retrieved from http://classics.mit.edu/Aristotle/rhetoric.1.i.html

Aronowitz, S., & Giroux, H. (1991). Textual authority. In M. W. Apple & L. K. Christian-Smith (Eds.), *The politics of the textbook* (pp. 213–241). New York, NY: Routledge.

Ayers, W. (1995). Interview with Maxine Greene. *Qualitative Studies in Education, 8*(4), 319–328.

Ayers, W. (2006). Trudging toward freedom. In G. Ladson-Billings & W. Tate (Eds.), *Education research in the public interest: Social justice, action, and policy* (pp. 81–97). New York, NY: Teachers College Press.

Bakhtin, M. M. (1981). *The dialogic imagination: Four essays.* Austin, TX: University of Texas Press.

Baldwin, J., & Mead, M. (1971). *A rap on race.* Philadelphia, PA: Lippencott.

Barrett, P. (2004, September 4). Harbor as classroom. *The Wall Street Journal,* p. B1.

Bateson, M. C. (1989). *Composing a life.* New York, NY: Plume.

Benjamin, S. (Producer), &. Hakford, T. (Director). (2004). *Ray* [Motion picture]. USA: Universal Studios.

A Curriculum of Imagination in an Era of Standardization, pages 115–125
Copyright © 2013 by Information Age Publishing

Bernstein, L. (1976). *The unanswered question: Six talks at Harvard.* Cambridge, MA: Harvard University Press.

Big Picture Company. (2006). *Our Mission.* Retrieved from http://www.bigpicture.org/

Billig, M. (1997). Keeping the white queen in play. In M. Fine, L. Weis, L. C. Powell, & L. M. Wong (Eds.), *Off white: Readings on race, power, and society* (pp. 149–157). New York, NY: Routledge.

Black, E. (2003). *War against the weak: Eugenics and America's plan to create a master race.* New York, NY: Four Walls Eight Windows.

Black, M. (1954/1955). Metaphor. *Proceedings of the Aristotelian Society, 55,* 273–294.

Breslin, J. (1993). *Mark Rothko.* Chicago, IL: University of Chicago Press.

Buber, M. (1974). *I and thou.* New York, NY: MacMillan.

Carlyle, T. (1859). *On heroes, hero-worship, and the heroic in history; six lectures.* New York, NY: Wiley & Halsted.

Center for Media Literacy. (2002). About CML: Educational philosophy. Retrieved from http://www.medialit.org/about-cml

Changeux, J., & Connes, A. (1995). *Conversations on mind, matter, and math.* Princeton, NJ: Princeton University Press.

Charron, K. H. (2009). *Freedom's teacher: The life of Septima Clark.* Chapel Hill, NC: University of North Carolina Press.

Chatwin, B. (1987). *The songlines.* London, England: Picador.

Chomsky, N. (1959). A review of B. F. Skinner's verbal behavior. *Language, 35,* 26–58.

Clarke, B. (2004, September 23). *Leaving children behind.* Corpwatch.org. Retrieved from http://www.corpwatch.org/article.php?id=11543

Conant, J. B. (1959). *The American high school today.* New York, NY: McGraw-Hill.

Connelly, F. M., & Clandinin, D. J. (1988). *Teachers as curriculum planners: Narratives of experience.* New York, NY: Teachers College Press.

Copland, A. (1932). *Piano variations* [Musical Score]. Cos Cob, CT: Cos Cob Press.

Coreil, C. (2003). *Schmoos, the lady of the evening and neglected ears.* Paper presented at the Imaginative Education Research Group Conference, Vancouver.

Croce, B. (1972). *Aesthetic.* New York, NY: Farrar.

Davidson, M. (2002). Hearing things: The scandal of speech in deaf performance. In S. L. Snyder, B. J. Brueggemann, & R. Garland-Thomson (Eds.), *Disability studies: Enabling the humanities* (pp. 76–87). New York, NY: MLA.

De Tocqueville, A. (1966). *Democracy in America.* (G. Lawrence, Trans.). New York, NY: Harper & Row. (Original work published 1844).

Delegates urge wider practice of sterilization. (1934, January 16). *Richmond Times-Dispatch.*

Delpit, L. (1995). I just want to be myself: Discovering what students bring to school "in their blood." In W. Ayers (Ed), *To become a teacher: Making a difference in children's lives.* New York, NY: Teachers College Press.

Denzin, N., & Lincoln, Y. (2003). *The landscape of qualitative research.* Thousand Oaks, CA: Sage.

Dewey, J. (1897). *My pedagogic creed*. Retrieved from http://www.infed.org/archives/e-texts/e-dew-pc.htm

Dewey, J. (1916). *Democracy and education*. New York, NY: Free Press.

Dewey, J. (1933). *How we think: A restatement of the relation of reflective thinking educative process*. Boston, MA: D.C. Heath. (Original work published 1910)

Dewey, J. (1934). *Art as experience*. New York, NY: Perigee Books.

Dewey, J. (1958). *Experience and nature*. New York, NY: Dover. (Original work published 1925).

Dickey, C. (1998). *Summer of deliverance: A memoir of father and son*. New York, NY: Touchstone.

Dickinson, E. (1914). Poem #27. In *The Single Hound: Poems of a Lifetime* (p. 30). Boston, MA: Little, Brown.

Dillon, S. (2006, March 26). Schools cut back subjects to push reading and math. *New York Times*. Retrieved from www.newyorktimes.com

Donne, J. (1839). *The works of John Donne* (Vol. 3; Henry Alford, Ed.). London, England: John W. Parker.

Driessen, M., & Morales, M. (2000). *The central Kansas virtual field trip*. Emporia, KS: Emporia State University Earth Science Department. Retrieved from http://www.emporia.edu/earthsci/outreach/ckft.html

Dylan, B. (1965). It's alright, Ma, (I'm only bleeding). On *Bringing it all back home* [Vinyl record]. New York, NY: Columbia Records.

Egan, K. (1992). *Imagination in teaching and learning: The middle school years*. Chicago, IL: The University of Chicago Press.

Egan, K. (1997). *The educated mind: How cognitive tools shape our understanding*. Chicago, IL: University of Chicago Press.

Eisner, E. W. (1985). *The art of educational evaluation: A personal view*. London, England: Falmer.

Eisner, E. W. (1994). *The educational imagination: On the design and evaluation of school programs*. Upper Saddle River, NJ: Prentice Hall.

Eisner, E. W. (1998a). *The enlightened eye: Qualitative inquiry and the enhancement of educational practice*. Upper Saddle River, NJ: Merrill.

Eisner, E. W. (1998b). *The kind of schools we need: Personal essays*. Portsmouth, NH: Heinemann.

Eisner, E. W. (2005). *Reimagining schools: The selected works of Elliot W. Eisner*. New York, NY: Routledge.

Eliot, T. S. (1943). *Four Quartets*. New York, NY: Harcourt Brace.

Fancher, R. (1985). *The intelligence men: Makers of the IQ controversy*. New York, NY: Norton.

Featherstone, J. (1995). Letter to a young teacher. In W. Ayers (Ed.), *To become a teacher: Making a difference in children's lives*. New York, NY: Teachers College Press.

Fitz-Enz, J. (2000). *The ROI of human capital: Measuring the economic value of employee performance*. New York, NY: Amacom Books.

Frank, A., Frank, O. M., & Presser, M. (1991). *Anne Frank: The diary of a young girl.* New York, NY: Doubleday.

Freire, P. (1970). *Pedagogy of the oppressed.* New York, NY: Seabury.

Freire, P. (1974). *Education for critical consciousness.* New York, NY: Seabury.

Freire, P. (1989). *Learning to question: pedagogy of liberation.* New York, NY: Continuum.

Freire, P. (1994). *Pedagogy of hope: Reliving pedagogy of the oppressed.* New York, NY: Continuum.

Freire, P. (1996). *Letters to Cristina: Reflections on my life and work.* New York, NY: Routledge.

Freire, P. (1997). *Pedagogy of the heart.* New York, NY: Continuum

Freire, P. (1998). *Pedagogy of freedom: Ethics, democracy, and civic courage.* Lanham, MD: Rowman & Littlefield.

Freire, P., & Freire, A. M. (1992). *Pedagogy of hope: Reliving pedagogy of the oppressed.* New York, NY: Continuum.

Freire, P., & Macedo, D. (1987). *Literacy: Reading the word & the world.* South Hadley, MA: Bergin & Garvey.

Freire, P., & Macedo, D. (1995). A dialogue: Culture, language and race. *Harvard Educational Review, 65*(3), 377–403.

Gallas, K. (2003). *Imagination and literacy: A teacher's search for the heart of learning.* New York, NY: Teacher's College Press.

Gardner, H. (1999). *Intelligence reframed: Multiple intelligence for the 21st century.* New York, NY: Basic Books.

Gates, H. L. (1992). *Loose cannons: Notes on the culture wars.* New York, NY: Oxford University Press.

Gay, G. (2000). *Culturally responsive teaching: Theory, research, & practice.* New York, NY: Teachers College Press.

Gaughan, J. (1997). *Cultural reflections: Critical teaching and learning in the English. classroom.* Portsmouth, NH: Boynton/Cook.

Georgia Department of Education. (2008). *Quality core curriculum.* Retrieved from https://georgiastandards.org/Standards/Pages/QCC.aspx

Giroux, H. (1988). *Teachers as intellectuals: Toward a critical pedagogy of learning.* South Hadley, MA: Bergin & Garvey.

Gladwell, M. (2002). *The tipping point: How little things can make a big difference.* Boston, MA: Back Bay.

Gladwell, M. (2005). *Blink: The power of thinking without thinking.* New York, NY: Little, Brown.

Goddard, H. (1920). *Human efficiency and levels of intelligence.* Princeton, NJ: Princeton University Press.

Google. (2011). Imagination. *NGram Viewer.* Retrieved from http://ngrams.googlelabs.com/graph?content=imagination&year_start=1800&year_end=2010&corpus=0&smoothing=2

Greene, M. (1978). *Landscapes of learning.* New York, NY: Teachers College Press.

Greene, M. (1988). *The dialectic of freedom.* New York, NY: Teachers College Press.

Greene, M. (1993). The passions of pluralism: Multiculturalism and the expanding community. *Educational Researcher, 22*(1), 13–18

Greene, M. (1995). *Releasing the imagination.* San Francisco, CA: Jossey-Bass.

Greene, M. (2001). *Variations on a blue guitar.* New York, NY: Teachers College Press.

Greene, M. (2008). In search of a critical pedagogy. In A. Darder, M. Baltodano, & R. D. Torres (Eds.), *Critical pedagogy reader: Theory and practice* (2nd ed., pp. 97–112). New York, NY: Routledge.

Greene, J., & Winters, M. (2005). Public high school graduation college readiness rates: 1991-2001. *Education working.* Paper No. 8. Retrieved from http://www.manhattan-institute.org/html/cr_baeo.htm

Gussow, M. (2000, September, 23).Yehuda Amichai, poet who turned Israel's experience in verse, dies at 76. *New York Times*, p. A14.

Gutstein, E. (2006). *Reading and writing the world with mathematics: Toward a pedagogy for social justice.* New York, NY: Routledge Falmer.

Hadamard, J. (1945). *An essay on the psychology of invention in the mathematical field.* Princeton, NJ: Princeton University Press.

Hawkes, T. (1972). *Metaphor.* London, England: Methuen.

He, M. F. (2003). *A river forever flowing: Cross-cultural lives and identities in the multicultural landscape.* Greenwich, CT: Information Age Publishing.

He, M. F., Phillion, J., Chan, E., & Xu, S. J. (2008). Immigrant students' experience of curriculum. In F. M. Connelly, M. F. He, & J. Phillion (Eds.), *Handbook of curriculum and instruction* (pp. 219–239). Thousand Oaks, CA: Sage.

Heidegger, M. (1947). Letter on humanism. In D. F. Krell (Ed.), *Basic writings* (p. 202). London, England: Routledge & Kegan.

Henle, M. (1986). *1879 and all that: Essays in the theory and history of psychology.* New York, NY: Columbia University Press.

Herrnstein, R., & Murray, C. (1994). *The bell curve: Intelligence and class structure in American life.* New York, NY: Simon & Schuster.

Hestor, M. (1967). *The meaning of poetic metaphor.* Paris, France: Moulton.

Hitler, A. (1925). *Mein Kamf.* Retrieved from http://www.hitler.org/writings/Mein_Kampf/mkv1ch11.html.

Hobbes, T. (2004). *The leviathan.* Whitefish, MT: Kessinger (Original work published 1834).

hooks, b. (1994). *Teaching to transgress: Education as the practice of freedom.* New York, NY: Routledge.

Horton, M., & Freire, P. (1990). *We make the road by walking.* Philadelphia, PA: Temple University Press.

Huxley, A. (1937). *Ends and means: An inquiry into the nature of ideas and into the methods employed for their realization.* London, England: Chatto & Windus/New York, NY: Harper & Brothers.

Igoa, C. (1995). *The inner world of the immigrant child.* New York, NY: St. Martin's.

Ikeda, D., with Nemoto, M. (1979). *On the Japanese classics: Conversations and appreciations.* (B. Watson, Trans.). New York, NY: Weatherhill.

Ikeda, D., with Gorbachev, M. (2005). *Moral lessons of the twentieth century*. London, England: I. B. Tauris Publishers.

Ikeda, D., with Boulding, E. (2010). *Into full flower: Making peace cultures happen*. Cambridge, MA: Dialogue Path Press.

Jackson, P. (2002). *John Dewey and the philosopher's task*. New York, NY: Teachers College Press.

James, W. (1890). *Principles of psychology*. New York, NY: Henry Holt.

Johnson, M. (1981). *Philosophical perspectives on metaphor*. Minneapolis, MN: University of Minnesota Press.

Johnson, M. (Producer), & Levinson, B. (Director). (1988). *Rain Man* [Motion picture]. USA: United Artists.

Johnson, R. K., & Swain, M. (1997). *Immersion education: International perspectives*. Cambridge, England: Cambridge University Press.

John-Steiner, V. (1985). *Notebooks of the mind*. Albuquerque, NM: University of New Mexico Press.

Kliebard, H. (1986). *The struggle for the American curriculum: 1893–1958*. Boston, MA: Routledge and Kegan Paul.

Kopelson, A. (Producer), & Davis, A. (Director). (1993). *The fugitive* [Motion picture]. USA: Warner Brothers.

Kress, T. M., & Lake, R. L. (2012). *We saved the best for you: Letters of hope, imagination and wisdom to 21st century educators*. Rotterdam: The Netherlands: Sense Publishers

Kuhn, T. (1962). *The structure of scientific revolutions*. Chicago, IL: University of Chicago Press.

Lake, R. (2010). Living above walls. In R. Lake (Ed.), *Dear Maxine: Letters from the unfinished conversation with Maxine Greene*. New York, NY: Teacher's College Press.

Lake, R. (2012). *Dear Nel: Letters to Nel Noddings from circles of care*. New York, NY: Teacher's College Press.

Lakoff, G., & Johnson, M. (1999). *Philosophy in the flesh: The embodied mind and its challenge to western thought*. New York, NY: Basic Books.

Lakoff, G., & Johnson, M. (2003). *Metaphors we live by*. Chicago, IL: University of Chicago Press. (Original work published 1980)

Lawton, D. (1984). Metaphor and the curriculum. In W. Taylor (Ed.), *Metaphors of Education* (pp.79–90). London, England: Heinemann.

Levi, P. (1988). *The drowned and the saved*. New York, NY: Summit Books.

Levinas, E. (1998). *Entre nous: On thinking-of-the-other*. New York, NY: Columbia University Press.

Levitin, K. (1982). *One is not born a personality. Profiles of Soviet educational psychologists* (V. V. Davydov, Ed.). Moscow, Russia: Progress Publishers.

Littky, D., & Grabelle, S. (2002). *The big picture: Education is everyone's business*. Alexandria, VA: ASCD.

Lovin' Spoonful. (1965). Night Owl Blues on *Do you believe in magic* [Vinyl record]. New York, NY: Kama Sutra Records.

Lux, T. (1997). *New and selected poems: 1975–1995.* New York, NY: Houghton Mifflin.

Mager, R. F. (1962). *Preparing instructional objectives.* Palo Alto, CA: Fearon.

Makdisi, S. (1998). *Romantic imperialism, universal empire and the culture of modernity.* Cambridge, England: Cambridge University Press.

Mann, T. (1955). *Confessions of Felix Krull, confidence man.* New York, NY: Alfred A. Knopf.

Martin, J. R. (2002). *Cultural miseducation: In search of a democratic solution.* New York, NY: Teachers College Press.

McKeon, R. (Ed.). (1941). *Poetics. Introduction to Aristotle* (I. Bywater, Trans.). New York, NY: Random House.

McLaren, P. (1991). Decentering culture: Postmodernism, resistance, and critical pedagogy. In N. B. Wyner (Ed.), *Current perspectives on the culture of schools.* Boston, MA: Brookline.

McManus, E. (2001). *Black bondage in the North.* Syracuse, NY: Syracuse University Press.

MET Center. (2006). *Facts and data.* Retrieved from http://www.themetschool.org/about_facts

Miller, A. (1960). Death of a salesman. In T. Cole (Ed.), *Playwrights on Playwriting.* New York, NY: Hill and Wang.

Modell, A. (2003). *Imagination and the meaningful brain.* Boston, MA: MIT press.

Moffett, J. (1968). *Teaching the universe of discourse.* Boston, MA: Houghton Mifflin.

Mohanty, C. T. (2003). *Feminism without borders: Decolonizing theory, practicing solidarity.* Durham, NC: Duke University Press.

Montenegro, D. (1987). Yehuda Amichai: An interview. *The American Poetry Review, 16*(3), 15–20.

Moya, P. M. L., & Hames-Garcia, M. R. (2000). *Reclaiming identity: Realist theory and the predicament of postmodernism.* Berkeley, CA: University of California Press.

NEAP. (2010). *The nation's report card: National profile.* Retrieved from http://nces.ed.gov/nationsreportcard/pdf/main2009/2010458.pdf

Nieto, S. (2000). *Affirming diversity: The sociopolitical context of multicultural education.* New York, NY: Longman.

Oakeshott, M. (1962). The voice of poetry in the conversation of mankind. In M. Oakeshott, *Rationalism in politics and other essays* (pp. 197–247). London, England: Methuen.

Ohanian, S. (1999). *One size fits few: The folly of educational standards.* Portsmouth, NH: Heinemann.

Orr, D. (1994). *Earth in mind: On education, environment, and the human prospect.* Washington, DC: Island.

Orwell, G. (1946). *Animal farm.* New York, NY: Harcourt & Brace.

Orwell, G. (1949). *Nineteen eighty-four.* New York, NY: Harcourt & Brace.

Ozick, C. (1991). *Metaphor and memory.* New York, NY: Knoph.

Parmalee, P. Coble, R., & Swanson, M. (1985). Certification: Does it matter? *Journal of Teacher Education, 36*(3), 13–15.

Passmore, J. (1975). On teaching to be critical. In R. F. Dearden, P. H. Hirst, & R. S. Peters (Eds.), *Education and reason* (pp. 415–433). London, England: Routledge & Kegan Paul.

Percy, W. (1979). *The moviegoer.* New York, NY: Knoph Publishers.

Perry, T. (2005, September). Taking time: Beyond memorization: Using drama to promote thinking. *English Journal, 95*(1), 120–123.

Peters, T., & Waterman, R. (1982). *In search of excellence.* New York, NY: Harper Collins.

Pinar, W. F. (1972). Working from within. *Educational Leadership, 29*(4), 329–331.

Pinar, W. F. (Ed.). (1975). *Curriculum theorizing: The reconceptualists.* Berkeley, CA: McCutchan.

Pinar, W. F. (Ed.). (1998). *The passionate mind of Maxine Greene: "I am not yet."* London, England: Falmer.

Pinar, W. F. (2004). *What is curriculum theory?* Mahwah, NJ: Lawrence Erlbaum.

Pinar, W. F., & Grumet, M. (1976). *Toward a poor curriculum.* Dubuque, IA: Kendall/Hunt.

Pinar, W. F., Reynolds, W. M., Slattery, P., & Taubman, P. M. (1995). *Understanding curriculum: An introduction to the study of historical and contemporary curriculum discourses.* New York, NY: Peter Lang.

Plato. (n.d.). *Meno.* Retrieved from http://classics.mit.edu/Plato/meno.html

Pyle, E. (2005, May, 13). Te$t market. *The Texas Observer, 97*(10). Retrieved from www.texasobserver.org

Rampey, B.D., Dion, G.S., and Donahue, P.L. (2009). *NAEP 2008 trends in academic progress in reading and mathematics (NCES 2009-479).* Washington, DC: National Center for Education Statistics, Institute of Education Sciences, U.S. Department of Education.

Rasheed, S. (2007). *Creating a language of possibility: An existentialist curriculum of action.* Lanham, MD: University Press of America.

Reynolds, Q. (1950). *The Wright brothers: Pioneers of American aviation.* New York, NY: Random House.

Reynolds, W. (1989). *Reading curriculum theory: The development of a new hermeneutic.* New York, NY: Peter Lang.

Reynolds, W. (2003). *No child left untested and education left behind.* Paper presented at a meeting of the Georgia Educational Research Association, Savannah, Georgia.

Richards, I. A. (1936). *The philosophy of rhetoric.* Oxford, England: Oxford University Press.

Richardson, L. (2003). Writing: A method of inquiry. In N. Denzin & Y. Lincoln (Eds.), *Collecting and interpreting qualitative materials* (2nd ed., pp. 499–54). Thousand Oaks, CA: Sage.

Ricoeur, P. (1981). *Hermeneutics and the human sciences: Essays on language, action and interpretation.* (J. B. Thompson, Trans.). Cambridge, UK: Cambridge University Press.

Rosenblatt, L. (1995). *Literature as exploration.* New York, NY: MLA publications.

Sacks, P. (1999). *Standardized minds: The high price of America's testing culture and what we can do to change it.* Cambridge, MA: Perseus Books.

Sandburg, C. (1970). *The complete poems of Carl Sandburg.* New York, NY: Harcourt.

Schubert, W. H. (2009). *Love, justice and education: John Dewey and the utopians.* Charlotte, NC: Information Age Publishers.

Schubert, W. H., Lopez-Schubert, A. L., Thomas, T. P., & Carroll, W. M. (2002). *Curriculum books: The first hundred years.* New York, NY: Peter Lang.

Seeger, P., & Reiser, B. (1989). *Everybody says freedom.* New York, NY: Norton.

Shapiro, L. (1993). A science to her fiction. *Newsweek, 122*(2), 61.

Share, J., Jolls, T, & Thoman, E. (2005). *Five key questions that can change the world.* Los Angeles, CA: Center for Media Literacy.

Shaull, R. (2003). *Pedagogy of the oppressed.* New York, NY: Continuum.

Shor, I., & Freire, P. (1987). *A pedagogy for liberation: Dialogues on transforming education with Ira Shor and Paulo Freire.* New York, NY: Bergin & Garvey.

Sidorkin, A. M. (2002) *Learning relations: Impure education, deschooled schools & dialogue with evil.* New York, NY: Peter Lang.

Skinner, B. F. (1953). *Science and human behavior.* New York, NY: Simon & Shuster.

Sleeter, C. E. (1993). How white teachers construct race. In C. McCarthy & W. Crichlow (Eds.), *Race, identity and representation in education* (pp. 157–171). New York, NY: Routledge.

Spencer, K., & Olsson, S. (2002). Sparks fly, stereotypes fade, when Worldlink TV puts American teenagers and Arab teens "face to face." *News from WorldLinkTV.* Retrieved from http://www.linktv.org/sitecontent/press/pr_11_13_02.pdf

Stephens, J. (1920). *Irish fairy tales.* London, England: Macmillan.

Stevens, W. (1954). *The collected poems of Wallace Stevens.* New York, NY: Knoph.

Sturges, J. (Producer/ Director). (1963). *The great escape* [Motion picture]. USA: United Artists.

Taylor, J. (1991). The frozen man. *New moon shine.* [CD]. New York: Columbia.

Thomas, R. (1996, January 15). James E. B. Breslin, 60, poetry professor, dies. *The New York Times.*

Tolkien, J. R. (1954). *The fellowship of the ring.* London, England: George Allen.

Treffert, G. (2006). *Savant syndrome: Islands of genius.* Retrieved from http://www.wisconsinmedicalsociety.org/savant/kimpeek.cfm

Tyler, R.W. (1949). *Basic principles of curriculum and instruction.* Chicago, IL: University of Chicago Press.

USA.org. (2011). Demographics of the United States. Retrieved from http://www.usa.org/demographics/

U.S. Department of Education. (1994). *Goals 2000: Educate America act.* Retrieved from http://www2.ed.gov/legislation/GOALS2000/TheAct/index.html

U.S. Department of Education. (2001). *No child left behind.* Retrieved from http://www2.ed.gov/nclb/overview/intro/presidentplan/proposal.pdf

U.S. Department of Education. (2005). *No child left behind: Expanding the promise, guide to President Bush's FY 2006 Education Agenda.* Retrieved from http://www2.ed.gov/about/overview/budget/budget06/nclb/expanding-promise.pdf

U.S. Department of Education. (2009). *Race to the top.* Retrieved from: http://www2.ed.gov/programs/racetothetop/index.html

U.S. Department of Treasury. (2003). *The new color of money.* Retrieved from http://www.moneyfactory.gov/newmoney/

U.S. National Commission on Excellence. (1984). *A nation at risk: The full account.* Cambridge, MA: USA Research.

U.S. Patent and Trademark Office (2006). *U.S. patent statistics chart: Calendar years 1963–2004.* Retrieved from http://www.uspto.gov/go/taf/us_stat.htm

Vanderbilt University. (2008, October 3). Musicians use both sides of their brains more frequently than average people. *ScienceDaily.* Retrieved from http://www.sciencedaily.com/releases/2008/10/081002172542.htm

Vico, G. (1744). *The new science.* Ithaca, NY: Cornell University Press.

Walmsey, S. A. (1981). On the purpose and content of secondary reading programs: An educational ideological perspective. *Curriculum Inquiry, 11*(1), 73–91.

Warburg, A. (1995). *Images form the region of the Pueblo Indians of North America.* Ithaca, NY: Cornell University Press.

Warner, M. (2006, December 26). Author uncovers stories of Arabs helping Jews during Holocaust. *PBS News Hour* [Television broadcast]. Washington, DC: McNeil/Lehrer Productions.

Warnock, M. (1976). *Imagination.* London, England: Faber & Faber.

Weiss, M., Systra, C., & Slater, S. (1998). Dinner with Maxine. In W. Ayers & J. Miller (Eds.), *A light in dark times: Maxine Greene and the unfinished conversation* (pp. 22–32). New York, NY: Teachers College Press.

West, C. (1994). *Race matters.* New York, NY: Vintage Books.

Westbury, I., & Wilkof, N. J. (Eds.). (1978). *Science, curriculum, and liberal education: selected essays: Joseph J. Schwab.* Chicago, IL: University of Chicago Press.

Willis, G. H., & Schubert, W. H. (Eds.). (1991). *Reflections from the heart of educational inquiry: Understanding curriculum and teaching through the arts.* Troy, NY: Educators International Press.

Wilson, G., & Grylls, D. (1977). *Know your child's IQ.* London, England: Futura.

Wink, J. (2000). *Critical pedagogy: Notes from the real world.* New York, NY: Longman.

Winner, E., & Gardner, H. (1993). Metaphor and irony: Two levels of understanding. In A. Ortony (Ed.), *Metaphor and thought* (2nd ed., pp. 425–443). New York, NY: Cambridge University Press.

Winslow, L., & McCleery, K. (1998, May 6). *The NewsHour with Jim Lehrer.* [Television Broadcast]. Washington, DC: Public Broadcasting Service. Transcript

retrieved from http://www.pbs.org/newshour/bb/youth/jan-june98/
suicide_5-6.html

Wolfe, T. (1987). *Bonfire of the vanities.* New York, NY: Bantam.

Woolf, V. (1976). *Moments of being: Unpublished autobiographical writings.* (J. Schulkind, Ed.) Orlando, FL: Harcourt.

Zenderland, L. (1998). *Measuring minds: Henry Herbert Goddard and the origins of American intelligence testing.* London, England: Cambridge University Press.

Lightning Source UK Ltd.
Milton Keynes UK
UKOW06n1001101117
312411UK00003BA/125/P